THERESE

DOROTHY DAY

THERESE

TEMPLEGATE PUBLISHERS
SPRINGFIELD, ILLINOIS 62705

Therese — Fifth Printing 1991

© 1960, 1979 Dorothy Day

Templegate Publishers
302 East Adams Street
P.O. Box 5152
Springfield, IL 62705

ISBN 0-87243-090-1

Preface

The first time I heard the name of St. Therese of the Child Jesus and of the Holy Face (to give her her whole title), also known as Therese of Lisieux, the Little Flower, was when I lay in the maternity ward of Bellevue Hospital in New York. Bellevue is the largest hospital in the world, and doctors from all over the world come there. If you are poor you can have free hospital care. At that time, if you could pay anything, there was a flat rate for having a baby—thirty dollars for a ten days' stay, in a long ward with about sixty beds. I was so fortunate as to have a bed next to the window looking out over the East River so that I could see the sun rise in the morning and light up the turgid water and make gay the little tugs and the long tankers that went by the window. When there was fog it seemed as though the world ended outside my window, and the sound of fog horns haunted the day and the night.

As a matter of fact, my world did end at the window those ten days that I was in the hospital, because I was supremely happy. If I had written the greatest book, composed the greatest symphony, painted the most beautiful painting or carved the most exquisite figure, I could not have felt more the exalted creator than I did when they placed my child in my arms. To think that this thing of beauty, sighing gently in my arms, reaching her little mouth for my breast, clutching at me with her tiny beautiful hands, had come from my flesh, was my own child! Such a great feeling of happiness and joy filled me that I was hungry for Someone to thank, to love, even to worship, for so great a good that had been bestowed upon me. That tiny child was not enough to contain my love, nor could the father, though my heart was warm with love for both.

We were radicals and had no particular religious affiliations. If I was drawn to any "organized church" it was to the Catholic. I knew of such saints as St. Francis of Assisi, and St. Augustine, and William James in his *Varieties of Religious Experience* had introduced me to St. Teresa of Avila, that well traveled yet cloistered contemplative with her vigorous writing and her sense of humor.

"What are you going to name your baby," the girl in the next bed to mine asked me.

"Teresa," I told her. "Tamar Teresa. I have a dear friend whose husband is a Zionist, and she has a little girl named Tamar. It means little palm tree, in Hebrew."

"And Teresa is after the Little Flower?"

I had never heard of the Little Flower and she had never heard of Teresa of Avila. She was a Catholic, and although she didn't read much, she knew the outlines of the life of St. Therese of Lisieux. In her pocketbook where she kept her powder and lipstick, tissues and rosary beads, money to buy candy and the Daily News when the boy made his rounds, she also had a medal of the Little Flower. "Here, I will give it to you for your baby," she said. "Pin it on her."

I was some years from being a Catholic and I shied away from this evidence of superstition and charm-wearing. I wanted no such talisman. Besides, the baby might swallow it. The pin might come unloosed and pierce that tender flesh.

"But if you love someone you want something around you to remind you of them," the girl protested. So I took the medal, and after hearing of St. Therese as the young novice mistress in her far off convent of Lisieux in Normandy, who had died the year I was born, and whose sisters were still alive, I decided that although I would name my child after the older saint, the new one would be my own Teresa's novice mistress, to train her in the spiritual life. I knew that I wanted to have the child baptized a Catholic and I wanted both saints to be taking care of her. One was not enough.

The next time I heard of St. Therese of Lisieux was in 1928, a year after I had been baptized a Catholic. I was thirty years old. I had read the New Testament, the *Imitation of Christ*, St. Augustine, and had dipped into the writings of some of the saints William James had introduced me to. I had a daily missal, too, which presented a little biography of the saint of the day, commemorated in the Mass. I still knew nothing of modern saints. Perhaps, I thought, the days of saints had passed.

At that time I did not understand that we are all "called to be saints," as St. Paul puts it. Most people nowadays, if they were asked, would say diffidently that they do not profess to be saints, indeed they do not want to be saints. And yet the saint is the holy man, the "whole man," the integrated man. We all wish to be that, but in these days of stress and strain we are not developing our spiritual capacities as we should and most of us will admit that. We want to grow in love but do not know how. Love is a science, a knowledge, and we lack it.

My confessor at the time was Father Zachary, an Augustinian Father of the Assumption, stationed at the Church of Our Lady of Guadalupe on West Fourteenth Street. He was preparing me for Confirmation, giving me a weekly evening of instruction.

One day Father Zachary said to me, "Here is a book that will do you good." He had already given me Challoner's *Meditations* and the St. Andrew Missal. The book he now handed me was *The Little White Flower, the Story of a Soul*, an unbound book which had a tan cover with a not too attractive picture of a young nun with a sweet insipid face, holding a crucifix and a huge bouquet of roses. I was by now familiar with the statues of this little sister which were to be seen in every church. They always called her little, although it is said she was very tall, and completely emaciated when the last photographs of her were taken. She had a broad face, however, and her habit and cloak concealed how thin she was. She was very young and her writing seemed to me like that of a school girl. I wasn't looking for anything so simple and felt slightly aggrieved at Father Zachary. Men, and priests too, were very insulting to women, I thought, handing out what they felt suited their intelligence; in other words, pious pap.

I dutifully read *The Story of a Soul* and am ashamed to confess that I found it colorless, monotonous, too small in fact for my notice. What kind of a saint was this who felt that she had to practice heroic charity in eating what was put in front of her, in taking medicine, enduring cold and heat, restraint, enduring the society of mediocre souls, in following the strict regime of the convent of Carmelite nuns which she had joined at the age of fifteen? A splash of dirty water from the careless washing of a nun next to her in the laundry, was mentioned as a "mortification" when the very root of the word meant death, and I was reading in my Daily Missal of saints stretched on the rack, burnt by flames, starving themselves in the desert, and so on.

Anatole France had made me familiar with Thais and Paphnutius, who were more to my taste. Joan of Arc leading an army fitted more into my concept of a saint, familiar as I was with the history of labor with its martyrs in the service of their brothers. "Love of brother is to lay down one's life on the barricades, in revolt against the hunger and injustice in the world," I told Father Zachary, trying to convert him to my point of view. Living as we were, in time of world revolution, when, as I felt, the people of the world were rising to make a better world for themselves, I wondered what this new saint had to offer.

As a matter of fact, I was working at the time for the Anti-Imperialist League, a Communist Party affiliate with offices on Union Square. I had been given the job by a young Jewish intellectual whom I had known when he went to Columbia University and took part in the anticonscription campaign of the first world war, who went to Russia to attend the Third International, who was active in the party for some years and who was dismissed in one of the frequent party purges some years later. My companions on the job were two women, both of them former Catholics, who looked on me indulgently and felt that my "faith" was a neurotic aspect of my character and something quite divorced from my daily life.

One woman was an adventurous young widow with a child who was living with a Scotch party official who was always being sent around the world on various party missions. Sometimes we would hear that he was in India or in Russia, but when he was home he devoted himself to Elizabeth. One time when I was sick with a bad cold they came to see me with a little roast chicken and some ginger ale. They took rooms in the same old tenement I was living in (quite a few other radicals lived there) and Elizabeth baby-sat for me on Sunday mornings when I went to Mass. Jack is dead now and the last time I saw Elizabeth was in 1936 in South Chicago during the Steel strike when she was writing pamphlets for the party and helping run a soup kitchen.

The other woman was a tragic figure to me, because her child had been run over by a truck on the New York streets, and she herself was beginning to suffer with the cancer which eventually killed her. Her husband was a big Irishman whose radical career began as a miner out west when, during a strike, he had a dispute with a priest which led him and his brothers to leave the Church and join with the most radical element of the labor movement, the I.W.W., which later lost many of its members to the Communist Party. Bill was always being disciplined by the Party for drinking and irresponsible conduct, suffering suspensions from active duty every now and then. But he was an able and dramatic leader and valued by the party.

The work that Elizabeth, Mary and I were engaged in under the leadership of Manny Gomez was to publicize and raise funds for General Sandino, who was resisting American aggression in Nicaragua. Our marines were hunting him in the mountains, and the work of our committee was to raise funds and medical supplies. I did the publicity.

I was so new a Catholic that I was still working for this committee for some months after my Baptism, and I talked to Father Zachary about the work. "I am in agreement with it," I told him. "We should not be sending our marines to Nicaragua. I am in agreement with many of the social aims of Communism. 'From each according to his ability and to each according to his need.' "

Father Zachary could only quote Lenin to me, saying "Atheism is basic to Marxism." He was the gentlest of confessors with me who, at that time, was a female counterpart of Graham Greene's Quiet American, wanting to do good by violence.

But I did not feel he understood me when he gave me the life of St. Therese to read. What did she have to do with this world conflict, in which I in my way was involved?

I obtained other work which took me out of the Party work, I was engrossed with my child, and with earning a living, I saw more and more the basic oppositions between Catholicism and Marxism. But it took me a longer time to realize the unique position of Therese of Lisieux in the Church today.

After this book was written, the *Hidden Face,* by Ida Goerres, was published by Pantheon in 1958. I had been told long before that such a book had been published in German, and some of my friends had tried to dissuade me from writing another book on Therese. "The best book has been written. The last word said." But of course there is never a last word said about holiness, about examples of holiness in our time.

So *Therese* is coming out. It is written very much from my own point of view, emphasizing aspects of her life, and of her family's life, that interested me particularly. I owe much to the *Story of a Family,* by Stephane-Joseph Piat, O.F.M., published by Kenedy, from whose editors I received permission to quote extensively. I only hope my so quoting will lead to a great demand for the work so that it will be reissued, preferably in paper so that it will be accessible to thousands more. No other writer has emphasized the family of Therese more than Father Piat, and what a great debt of gratitude we owe him. Henri Gheon's *The Secret of the Little Flower;* Henri Petitot, O.P., *Spiritual Renascence;* the series by André Combes on various aspects of her teachings; Hans Urs von Balthasar, *Therese of Lisieux;* her life by Monsignor Laveille —these have been my source books. But most of all I have read her own writings: *The Story of a Soul;* her collected letters; *Novissima Verba* (her last words, collected by her sister Pauline); her poetry.

I have read Father Michael Day's translation of her life and that of Allan Beavers; the translation by Monsignor Ronald Knox is the most recent. He was asked by the Carmel of Lisieux to make the new translation, after the scholarly work of Father François de Sainte-Marie, O.C.D., in restoring and bringing out a facsimile edition of her work, had been finished. Permission had been given in Rome for the publication of the complete text in September, 1952. Her original work, written in three parts and addressed to her sister Pauline, to her Mother Prioress, and to her sister Marie, was combined and rearranged by her older sister, at Therese's request. Some of the editing and rearranging was not too happy and brought forth some very harsh criticism these last years, when theologians and intellectuals began to turn to the Little Flower for guidance, and found in her a depth of wisdom and holiness they had missed. I have had available a complete set of the books issued by Father Francois de Sainte-Marie: the facsimile edition of the notebooks, the concordance, the analysis of the changes made, etc.

As to Father Knox's translation, I do not believe that it was the best that could have been done. To my mind he thought of Therese as a little English school girl, and though I enjoyed his bringing out her humor and mischievousness (she said she did her best meditations lying in bed in the morning) I felt he often missed the point. I would rather have seen a translation by the English equivalent of an Ida Goerres, who gives credit to Therese's family and her sisters in Carmel, absolving them of the malice and stupidity and obtuseness and mediocrity which many of the critics in France have accused them of. She clears up to a great extent the mystery of Therese's illness in her childhood and she points with hope to the fulfillment of Therese's promise that she would pray always that God would build up a legion of "little" saints. She points constantly to the pleas of Therese that we have boundless confidence in God's infinite mercy and love. In these days of fear and trembling of what man has wrought on earth in destructiveness and hate, Therese is the saint we need.

I am afraid that one must not look for scholarship in this story of Therese. Between living in houses of hospitality and answering vast quantities of mail, and editing the paper, the *Catholic Worker,* I have not had time to go back and check sources; both the Taylor and Knox translations of her autobiography were used, and there was the same freedom of choice in the versions of Scripture that were used.

My purpose in writing the book in the first place was to reach some of the 65,000 subscribers to the *Catholic Worker,* many of whom are not Catholic and not even "believers," to introduce them to a saint of our day. Many of them are familiar only with a St. Francis of Assisi or a St. Joan of Arc. Also I wrote to overcome the sense of futility in Catholics, men, women, and youths, married and single, who feel hopeless and useless, less than the dust, ineffectual, wasted, powerless. On the one hand Therese was "the little grain of sand" and on the other "her name was written in heaven"; she was beloved by her heavenly Father, she was the bride of Christ, she was little less than the angels. And so are we all.

Contents

PART ONE

"The dearly loved garden of home"

I

Louis Martin

THE FATHERS of Louis Martin and Zelie Guerin, parents of the Little Flower, were military men. Louis was born in Bordeaux, but his family moved to Alençon, then to Strasbourg, and back once more to Alençon. Traveling as much as Louis Martin did as a child, he grew up with a love for travel, and, after his marriage and during his later life, he made many pilgrimages. The letters he wrote to his wife and daughters concerning his travels must have been of great interest.

There were relatives of the Martin family in Rennes, and in 1842 and 1843 young Louis went there to learn the trade of watchmaking with a cousin of his father. He loved Brittany "for the simplicity of manners, the wild poetry of its scenery, and the fire of its mystical temperament. He liked to wear the national costume and he studied its folklore. In his fine sonorous voice he liked to sing the songs of Brittany."

Recently, a friend of mine brought me a book filled with reproductions of the art of the Breton peasant. There were studies of shrines erected along the roads and in the public squares of the towns. Some of these shrines are massive and almost primitive stories in stone, depicting such scenes as Christ washing the feet of His disciples, the Last Supper, and Christ hanging from the cross on Calvary. By surrounding themselves with art of this type the Breton people gave expression to the strength of their belief. No wonder it was con-

sidered a high compliment when they said of Louis Pasteur
that he "had the faith of a Breton peasant."

Louis Martin was nineteen when he went to Rennes. When
he was twenty he visited the monastery of the Great St. Bernard, eight thousand feet up in the Alps, and made a retreat
there. Then he settled in Strasbourg, where there were more
relatives, and continued his study of clockmaking, which required a long apprenticeship. He stayed at Strasbourg with
a friend of his family, Aimé Mathey. Although the Matheys
were nominally Catholics, they never practiced their faith and
this, of course, was a matter of grief to Louis Martin. His
large-hearted warmth is indicated, it seems to me, in the con-
tinuation of his friendship with a family that regarded so
lightly the things he held most dear.

He lived with the Matheys for the two years of his apprenticeship, and these were very happy years. He walked all
over Alsace, and during one such walking trip, when he and
young Mathey were bathing in a stream, he saved the son of
the house from drowning.

In 1845 he journeyed from Strasbourg, partly by foot,
partly by coach, to the Swiss frontier, and paid a visit again
to the hermitage of the Great St. Bernard, this time to apply
for admittance to the order that conducts the hospice. The
priests there are called Canons Regular.

A canon lives in community and sings the praises of God
by the daily recitation of the Divine Office in choir, but he
is also prepared to preach and teach, administer the sacraments, tend the sick, and give hospitality to pilgrims and
travelers. According to its historians, the Order began at the
time of Christ Himself, dating from the Apostles. There were
many reforms, of course. Some regard St. Augustine as the
order's founder; some as its reformer or lawgiver. When a
controversy arose between the Benedictines and the Canons
Regular with regard to precedence, the question was settled
by Pius V in favor of the Canons, on account of their apostolic origin.

The Canons Regular whom visitors find serving at the

hospice of the Great St. Bernard are, however, usually called monks. This famous monastery was founded in the year 969 and was meant by the founder to be used for the convenience of pilgrims and travelers who crossed the Alps at a point which was always full of dangers. Perhaps it was the craving for adventure that led Louis Martin to this famous place. He had come from a family of military men and, according to Father Piat in the *Story of a Family,* he would have preferred a military career, "but now that Napoleon was dead, who was there for him to follow?" The desire for a leader is in us all, for a leader and a temporal cause, to match in grandeur the glimpses of the Absolute that come to us in rare flashes.

Louis Martin had always been a religious man, coming from an intensely religious home. The story is told of his soldier father that when some of his men in the army were astonished to see him so long on his knees after Mass he remarked, "It is because I believe."

The military atmosphere of his home undoubtedly had its reflection in Louis Martin's way of thinking, and it showed in his sense of responsibility and his attention to duty. There is about the French an exalted way of expressing themselves, a sense of reverence, a sense of awe. Perhaps the military background which gave Louis a world-view also enlarged his mind and made him meditate on the transcendence of God. On the other hand, his trade of watchmaking may have contributed to his sense of the immanence of God.

I have heard the Little Flower condemned because she came from a bourgeois atmosphere, because she lived always in comfortable surroundings. It is necessary to study her background and to call attention to the fact that her father was a man who had served seven years of apprenticeship as a watchmaker and who spent his life in that business until some time after his marriage. He had wanted to enter the Canons Regular and to spend his life in the joyous worship of God and in the hospitable love of his brother, with, perhaps, an occasional adventurous rescue of travelers for which the hospice is famous. But, rejected by the Canons Regular, not only because he did not know Latin or Greek, but also because of the ill health which attended his studies, he made up his mind to live a holy life in the world, earning his living as a gentleman should, by the sweat of his own brow rather than that of any one else's—and one can sweat quite as much over little things as over big things. A meticulous work like that of watchmaking can be more a strain on the nerves than any heavy manual labor.

Louis Martin lived in the days of the beginnings of revolutionary thought, of Kropotkin, whose thinking was shaped by the watchmakers of the Jura mountains where Louis himself studied. He lived in those vital years of 1850-1890 when Marxism and anarchism struggled for possession of the First International. He lived at the same time as Proudhon, the unMarxian socialist, as Father de Lubac, S.J., called him, who said "Property is theft." I have often wondered whether in his long years of apprenticeship Louis Martin ever engaged in discussion of the social problems of the day. I am sure that there must have been some talk of the revolution of 1848, of the condition of the working classes. There is one passage in Father Piat's book which might indicate that in Paris he came in contact with radical groups:

> The sojourn at Paris, after his Strasbourg years, which appears to have been prolonged for two or three years, was a strong test of Louis Martin's faith. The Voltairean spirit, which had ushered in the July Monarchy, still flourished in intellectual circles, despite the vigorous counter-offensive of Lacordaire and Montalembert. The ruling classes, obeying Guizot's order, "Get rich!" remained deaf to the murmurs of revolt that were rising from the working men. In vain did Frederic Ozanam raise the alarm. In order to draw attention to the danger to society, and the spiritual and material needs of the proletariat, the upheaval, bloodshed and barricades of the June days of 1848 would be needed. For the moment Paris gave itself up to scepticism and amusement.

> Louis Martin came very near to danger. Taking advantage of his natural generosity, some strangers invited him

to join a philanthropic club, apparently devoted to works of charity. He inquired more closely concerning them and discovered that the club was in reality a secret society. His loyal nature was indignant. He cared only for what was open and aboveboard. Only evil works seek for darkness. He firmly refused the acquaintanceship and preserved his freedom.

I wish Father Piat had told us more of this "club." Who were these "strangers"? Why are radicals more dangerous than the lukewarm, like Martin's friend Aimé Mathey? "I had rather you were hot or cold," Christ said. "The lukewarm I will spew out of my mouth."

The point I would like to make is that it is too bad that Father Piat paints in dark colors the attempts to work for the people at that time. I would like to know more of that secret society which he mentions as a temptation to Louis Martin. I do not think that it was only a question of "evil works" that he was avoiding.

In making this comment there is certainly implied no criticism of Louis Martin. I am only interested in thinking along these lines because of St. Therese's love for her father. It is partly because of this father, who played so great a role in her life, that she was what she was. When she told of her little way of dependence on God's merciful love she was thinking, too, of her dearly beloved father.

Louis Martin's vocation was a great one, although he was not to spend his days in the religious life or in a struggle to better social conditions. It was through marriage and the bringing up of a family that he was to play his great and saintly role in the world. I say saintly, although he has not been proclaimed a saint. There is a statue of him in the church in which he was baptized, just as there is a statue of the Little Flower's mother in her baptismal church to remind the faithful of these parents.

Louis Martin was tempted in other ways, as Father Piat indicates:

His personal charm exposed him to temptations of another sort. Later on he mentioned them to his wife in confidence and the latter profited thereby to put her young brother on his guard when he went to the capital to study medicine. "I am very anxious about you," she writes. "My husband utters gloomy forebodings daily. He knows Paris and he tells me you will be exposed to temptations which you will be unable to resist because you are not sufficiently religious. He has told me what he experienced himself and the courage he needed to emerge victorious from all these struggles. If you only knew what he has been through."

Louis Martin returned to Normandy after his years in Paris, to set up his business as a watch and clockmaker. Later he became owner of the house where he had his business. He loved his work and was not interested in marriage. He belonged to Church organizations devoted to charity, and his Sundays were given completely to the Church. Social functions had little attraction for him; his chief means of recreation were pilgrimages and long walks through the forests. He also loved to sit on the banks of a lake or stream fishing. Usually when he had fished all day he took his catch to the Convent of Poor Clares in Alençon.

Later on, his business flourished so that he bought a little piece of property known as the Pavillion—a place where he could keep his fishing tackle and where he could read and think at leisure. The property consisted of a hexagonal tower containing a ground floor and two upper stories to which access was gained by an outside staircase reaching as far as the terrace at the level of the first floor and then inside by a wooden spiral staircase. He had here only his books and his fishing tackle and guns for hunting. His Church, his work, and his recreation completely contented him for the next eight years of his life. He was thirty-five years old when he married Zelie Guerin.

II

Zelie Guerin

THE STORY of Zelie Guerin is not so happy a one. She was born in a village on the main road between Paris and Brest. Zelie's father was a soldier who used to tell her of the insurrections of the Republican troops during the revolution which occurred in his childhood, the locked and barred churches, the Masses celebrated in secret. His own uncle was a priest who had to be concealed once in the family homestead, and little Isidore Guerin, Zelie's father, was given the job of guiding him on his journeys around the countryside. Once, the priest had to hide in the kneading trough where he was able to escape the pursuing and searching soldiers only because of the presence of mind of the child, who sat on the lid of the trough and spread out his toys and played there. The priest-uncle was later imprisoned but released in 1835.

Isidore was drafted the day before his twentieth birthday. He saw active service and was decorated. When the Emperor Napoleon III fell, Isidore went back home, only to re-enlist. He was married at thirty-nine and had three children, Marie Louise, Zelie, and Isidore. The father was stern but loved by his daughters. The mother was severe, religious, and rigidly economical. Their circumstances were very difficult. The father had refused a captaincy because the commission meant more honor than profit.

"My childhood and youth," Zelie wrote afterwards in a letter to her brother, "were shrouded in sadness, for if our

9

mother spoiled you, to me, as you know, she was too severe. Good as she was, she did not know how to treat me, so that I suffered deeply." But Zelie had great comfort in her sister, Marie Louise.

Many years ago I read Balzac's *Eugenie Grandet*, and it tells the story of a girl in a household where there was such parsimony that all the food was locked up to be doled out by the ounce from day to day. The book returns to my memory when I read of the economies of Zelie's mother. She and her husband were able to save enough money from a soldier's pay to enable Isidore, upon his retirement after thirty-five years of service, to buy a comfortable little home in Alençon.

So there in Alençon we have these two families living— the Martins and the Guerins—and both of them owning their own homes. The pension of Isidore Guerin was 297 francs a year. He occupied himself with working in wood and his wife opened a little café. The story is that she was so fond of sermonizing her customers that the café was a failure and was given up.

The schools were very good in Alençon and Isidore Guerin was anxious that his daughters be well educated. They attended an academy taught by the Religious of the Sacred Hearts of Jesus and Mary and of the Perpetual Adoration of the Blessed Sacrament. These Religious were generally known as the Picpus Congregation, so named because the community was started in a street in Paris, called the Rue Picpus, during the Revolution.

Zelie had a close friendship with her sister. Both girls grew up with a desire to enter the religious life, but Zelie, when she applied for admission to the convent, was refused. It seemed to be one of those arbitrary acts which come so often in our lives, which disconcert us, for which we see no reason. One would think that a young, healthy, pious girl who came from a hard-working family would be received with open arms by a community of teaching nuns. There is always talk about the need for vocations. And yet here she was turned down, without rhyme or reason. Such a refusal must have meant a grave humiliation for the young girl. She must have wondered what there was in her that made the Mother Superior refuse her admittance. It shows, however, her complete acceptance of the will of God, her "abandonment to Divine Providence," that she took the refusal with no rebellion and certainly with no sense of failure.

Surely this rejection was an example of the sowing spoken of in the Gospel. The Superior, with some deep intuition, sowed this good seed in the world, and later other convents reaped a great harvest—five young women, and one of them a canonized saint.

Zelie prayed humbly: "Lord, since, unlike my sister, I am not worthy to be your bride, I will enter the married state in order to fulfil Your holy will. I beg of You to give me many children and to let them all be consecrated to You."

Thereupon she set about making a living in the world. The story is that she heard a voice telling her to apprentice herself to the makers of Alençon lace, for which the town is famous. There is no reason to doubt that she received such guidance. I think many of us when in a quandary as to what course to take, turn to prayer, with the immediate result that we know which way to turn, what course to take, even in such practical matters as earning a living.

It is interesting that Zelie undertook, like Louis Martin, a fine and delicate work. He turned to his watchmaking, and she to her lacemaking, both of them doing work which required absorption and attention, fine and meticulous work, slow work which could not be accomplished in a day, work made up of little moves, little stitches, to accomplish the finished product, a work which depended on faith as well as will and perseverance to complete the task.

Each lacemaker, when she had completed her apprenticeship in a school, could work at home on her specialty, and a true master of the craft was taught to co-ordinate and correct and combine the work of the other lacemakers and produce the finished product. Zelie studied for a number of years and became so skilled that she opened an office in her home. "I am never happier," she wrote in one of her letters, "than when sitting at my window assembling my Point d'Alencon lace."

The lace for which Alençon is famous was introduced to the town as a craft in 1664, thirty skilled workers having been brought from Venice to start the industry. The lace is made of very fine handspun linen thread and worked by the needle into lace pieces of around one third of an inch in length and joined together by imperceptible stitches. Once there were over eight thousand women stitching this beautiful French lace, now only a few workers in a convent in Alencon continue this skill. Where there is originality of design, some pieces take as much as thirty-five hours of most careful stitching.

It was this work of finishing, the most difficult of all, that Zelie undertook. Her employees worked in their own homes, and she supplied the designs, assembled the work, and obtained the orders. Her work was considered the best in the country and often sold for five hundred francs a meter, which is about 39 inches. At five francs to the dollar, this would have amounted to one hundred dollars a yard. A luxury item indeed! But it was beautiful work to occupy the time one has to spend earning a living. There are not many lacemakers left in the western world today.

For ten years, between 1853 and 1863, she worked for the Paris firm of Pigache. Her sister, Marie Louise, went to Paris to arrange the business details for her. This older sister who later played a great part in the education of the two oldest Martin girls, her nieces, suffered not only from frail health but also from scruples. She was taught to read in the Apocalypse, she was rigid in the performance of her religious duties, and she suffered from her scruples for many years—a mental suffering which contributed to her poor health. She also took upon herself a burden of corporal penances which exhausted her.

The Little Flower must have known well what scrupulosity and harshness can do to the religious life when she proclaimed her faith and confidence in the all-merciful love of God. Yet she was known for her meticulous attention to duty, the stress she laid on the little way of spiritual childhood, the offering to God of little sacrifices which meant constant attention, constant practice of the presence of God; but she also stressed the childlike confidence, the lack of self-importance which saved one from undue grief over lapses and failures.

When in 1858 Marie Louise was accepted by the Visitation nuns at Le Mans, Zelie began to think more often of marriage. She is described as being below middle height, with brown hair and black eyes, a well-shaped nose, altogether a pretty face. Sometimes there was a shade of sadness in the eyes. But generally there was a vivacity and good nature that made her very attractive.

Meanwhile, Louis Martin's mother was anxious to see him married. She was also attending some of the classes with Zelie in lacemaking and so became acquainted with the young woman; she made up her mind that here was a proper wife for her son.

A meeting which Zelie had with Louis Martin on the bridge of St. Leonard made the understanding between the two women easier. Zelie was crossing the bridge on an errand when her attention was caught by this tall, grave man of thirty-five. Perhaps their eyes met. Perhaps a glance was exchanged. Perhaps they "knew" each other, in the sense that an immediate sense of intimacy sprang up between them. For a second time Zelie heard a voice speaking to her, again on a most practical matter. "This is the man you are going to marry."

It was the mother who saw to it that the young people were brought together, and within three months the marriage took place at the Church of Notre Dame, on Tuesday, July 13, 1858, at midnight. It was not an unusual custom at that time for weddings to take place at that hour.

The Martin house was large enough to have two families live separately, and there was still space for the workshop and the jewelry store.

Zelie brought her husband a dowry of five thousand francs and seven thousand francs saved from her personal earnings. Louis Martin owned two properties both free from debt and furnished, his business, and twenty-two thousand francs.

III

Marriage

AND NOW COMES a strange part of their story, difficult to understand in this modern day. In spite of the love which Louis Martin must have felt for Zelie Guerin, he felt himself still called to the celibate life. He recognized Zelie's purity and spirit of sacrifice, and so he hoped to have a companionship and a love which was entirely spiritual. And with the consent of their spiritual director this was the kind of adventure they embarked on.

There is no knowing how Zelie felt, she who had desired to marry in order to have children to give to God. From the warmth of the letters which she wrote later, it can easily be seen that she was much in love, but at the time satisfied with the tenderness and affection which until then she had received only from her sister; undoubtedly reverencing the man she had chosen to spend her life with, it was probably not easy for her to broach the subject of her desires. According to Father Piat she understood the mystery of life only incompletely: "The problem of sexual initiation did not belong to the order of the day. It was a subject banished from consideration in schools, and was supposed to be forbidden to the curiosity of young people in the hermetically sealed circles of the Catholic middle class."

The Guerin family were particularly austere. Certainly there was no frankness between mother and daughter. When

15

the ordinary physical facts of sex were explained to Zelie before her wedding, a sense of physical shock inclined her for
the time to her husband's way of thinking. The two went to
the Visitation Convent to see her sister on their wedding day,
and the sight of Marie Louise, "the soul of her soul" as she
had called her, so happy in religious life, aroused again in
Zelie a longing for the convent. Nineteen years later, in a
letter to her daughter Pauline, "the one she loved, the one
who drew her most," as Therese wrote years later, Mrs.
Martin said:

> I can say that I had my cry out, that day. I cried as I had
> never cried in my life and as I was never to cry again. My
> poor sister did not know how to comfort me. For all that
> I was not grieving at seeing her there; on the contrary I
> should have liked to be there also. I compared my life with
> hers, and my tears flowed more than ever. In short, for a
> very long while my thoughts were in the Visitation. I often
> went to see my sister and there I breathed a peace and
> calm which I could not describe. When I returned home,
> I felt so unhappy at being in the world, that I yearned to
> hide myself and share her life.
>
> You, Pauline, who love your father so much, will think,
> perhaps, that I was making him unhappy and that I had
> spoilt our wedding day for him. But no, he understood
> me and consoled me as well as he could, for he had similar
> inclinations. I even think that our mutual affection was
> increased. We always thought alike, and he was always my
> comfort and support.

Zelie joined with her husband in all his charities, and in
addition to her own lacemaking, and her care of the home,
she undertook for some years the care of a five-year-old child
who had lost his mother.

For ten months, Louis and Zelie lived a celibate life, and
then the intervention of a confessor changed their attitudes.
They began to see more clearly that the marriage act was not
only for self-gratification and procreation but for the mutual
sanctification of husband and wife, a physical expression of

that nuptial love, that great mystery, which is a sample of the love of God for man.

Later on, the Little Flower went through an analogous struggle. At the process of canonization, her sister Marie told that the child of nine could not bear to be undressed for baths. The Little Flower herself wrote that she was troubled at having a body: "I was not at ease in it, I was ashamed of it."

In view of the fact that she was a child of remarkable beauty this is a statement that can bear some deep pondering. Most children's vanity and self-love is developed at an early age, so that their little self-conscious ways, their airs and graces, their affectations, indicate a consciousness of the body and their pleasure with it. They are at ease in the flesh. Later, with the growth of love, real love, there comes a consciousness of sex which makes one displeased with the body and its limitations. There is a troubled self-consciousness then, a feeling of the heaviness of the flesh, the crudity of it, the rawness of such material to express so great, so sublime an emotion as love. The holier the person, the more he is weighed down by the misery of the flesh with its desires and concupiscences. Together with pride of life comes an understanding of our inadequacy to express all that is in our hearts. Perhaps, too, most children raised in the city are too far removed from the natural animal functioning of life.

Later, Therese came to understand and think more nobly of the relations between soul and body. Her sister Pauline, Mother Agnes, the "little mother" who helped raise her, made the following statement at the process of canonization:

The servant of God was very simple, completely ignorant of evil, and afraid of discovering it, as she acknowledges in her autobiography. She had entrusted the safeguarding of her purity to the Blessed Virgin and St. Joseph. Later on, she learnt that to the pure all things are pure. When I saw that she was informed concerning the facts of life, I asked her who had given her this knowledge. She replied that, without seeking for it, she had found it out for herself in nature, by watching the flowers and the birds, and she added:

"But our Lady knew everything fully. Did she not ask the Angel on the day of the Annunciation, 'How shall this be done, seeing that I know not man?' It is not the knowledge of things that is evil. Everything that God has made is very good and noble. For those whom God calls to that state, marriage is a beautiful thing. It is sin which disfigures and defiles it."

Mrs. Martin finished the letter in which she spoke of her sadness on her wedding day by telling her daughter how happy she was when the children began to arrive. "Our ideas changed somewhat," she writes. "Thenceforward we lived only for them. They made all our happiness and we would never have found it save in them. In fact, nothing more cost us anything; the world was no longer a burden to us. As for me, my children were my great compensation, so that I wished to have many in order to bring them up for Heaven."

The first three children were Marie Louise, Marie Pauline, and Marie Leonie. The Martins had resolved to name all the children after the Blessed Mother regardless of sex. Of course the second and third children were called by their second names, Pauline and Leonie, and only the first was called Marie. The first two children thrived. Leonie, a little blonde, was delicate and slow from the first, and caused her mother much worry. She began to know the anguish of a mother.

Many of the letters which Mrs. Martin wrote at this time were to her sister-in-law, the wife of Isidore. How I would like to see them all collected together. "Little Leonie is over nine months old now and is not nearly so steady on her feet as Marie was at three months. The poor child is very delicate. She has a sort of chronic whooping cough."

Zelie was able to nurse these first three children. When the fourth arrived, Marie Helene, she was not able to nurse her and had to look around for a wet nurse, a difficult thing, since her husband had to be completely satisfied as to the moral character of the woman who was to nurse his baby. By this time he felt that the physical was so bound up with the spiritual that a sensitive infant could be harmed by the very milk of a woman who had not a good moral character. At this time too, Mrs. Martin discovered a lump in her breast, the first sign of a cancer which was to cause her death when she was forty-five. She did not receive the immediate attention that one would receive today, and nothing was done. The baby was put out to nurse in the country and Zelie writes:

Last Tuesday, I went to see my little Helene. I set off alone at seven in the morning, in rain and wind which accompanied me there and back. Imagine how tired I was on the road, but I was upheld by the thought of soon holding my treasure in my arms. She is a dainty little jewel, enchantingly pretty.

I never remember experiencing such a thrill of happiness as when I took her in my arms, and she smiled so charmingly at me that I seemed to be looking at an angel. In short, I cannot describe it. I do not think I have ever yet seen, or will ever see again such an enchanting little girl. Oh, when shall I have the pleasure of possessing her completely! I cannot realize that I have the honor to be the mother of such a delightful little creature. Oh indeed, I do not repent of having married. If you had seen how well the two elder ones looked in their pretty frocks. Everyone admired them and could not help looking at them. And I was radiant, and saying to myself, "They are mine. I have still two others who are not here, one pretty and one less pretty, whom I love as much as the others, though she will not do me so much credit."

She was supremely happy with her four children and when she heard of a mother having triplets, she cried out with envy. She wrote often to her brother, telling him of the development of her children. Isidore, now happily settled and married at Lisieux, was godfather to Pauline, the second child, and Zelie wrote how fond the little girl was of dress, how she boasted of her godfather's beard, how affectionate she was. "You do not know how attractive and caressing she is. She kisses you every few minutes, without being told to do so. She blows kisses to 'the good Jesus.' "

It must be remembered that Zelie had a house to care for, with one servant to help her. She also kept to her lacemaking, and yet she had time to devote herself to her little ones. As she said, she and her husband lived for them.

On the subject of the children, Father Piat writes:

Mme. Martin has left us something better than a learned work, namely a human document; the admirable correspondence wherein she sets down day by day, her impressions, her plans and her dreams. There are about two hundred letters, which her daughters carefully collected and which range from January, 1863, to August 16, 1877. She wrote to her brother, to his wife, to her sister, and to her two daughters when they were at boarding school. She sent to them what she calls "some sparks from the hearth." Her husband did not write letters, but left that to his wife. The letters that are lost are those to her older sister, and to judge from what she says to her brother, this is a great loss. "If you could see the letter I have written to my sister at Mans, you would be jealous. There are five pages. But I say things to her which I do not tell you. We talk to each other of a mysterious, angelic world, above the mire of this earth."

Father Piat regrets the too radical detachment which meant that the nun put all of her sister's letters into the fire. However, knowing nuns as we do, I wonder where she would have kept so evidently voluminous a correspondence.

When Isidore had been in Paris before his marriage, Zelie begged him to go to Our Lady of Victories and say a Hail Mary to her. She told him that she had received graces from Our Lady which she alone knew. She sent him "potted goose and jam." He gave her plenty of occasion to worry because he fell in love with a woman who was frivolous and indifferent to him. Zelie writes to tell him what kind of a wife he ought to be looking for:

You are still thinking about Mlle. X it seems. I think you are crazy, I am persuaded of it. You will come to grief, either over her or over somebody else, for the only considerations that weigh with you are futile ones: beauty and money. You do not trouble yourself about the qualities that make a husband's happiness or the defects that cause his sorrow and ruin. As you know, all that glitters is not gold. The principal thing is to seek out a real home-making woman, who is not afraid to soil her hands with work and cares for dress only as much as it must be cared for; who knows how to train her children to labor and piety. Such a woman would frighten you. She would not be brilliant enough in the eyes of the world; but sensible men would love her better with nothing, than another with a dowry of 50,000 francs who lacks the qualities I have mentioned.

In 1865, the year following this letter, Isidore suddenly gave up the idea of trying to be a doctor and decided to be a pharmacist at Lisieux, 170 miles away. Zelie had wanted him to set up his practice near her at Alençon or at Le Mans, near his sister who was a nun. She was very much upset at this change in his plans. She was "overwhelmed with business orders and had four children on her hands," at this time. "Then I must say goodbye for good," she wrote. "We shall hardly see each other again save in the next world. I shall never in my poor life, which I do not think will be very long, have time to go to see you. . . . I shall look at your photograph which is a very poor consolation. . . . However, that must not make you take the wrong road. You must settle where you have reason to think you can build up a good business."

The move was all for the best, and the business which he purchased, a large shop on premises which had been used by apothecaries and chemists since 1550 and was at that time owned by the Fournet family, prospered. The next year he married the daughter of the house, Celine, after whom one of the Martin daughters was named.

Isidore's bride was nineteen years old and was related to

the best families in the neighborhood. In addition to great
sweetness and piety, she possessed a surprising maturity of
judgment and a moral balance. Zelie loved her at once and
happily received her at her home after their marriage, before
they returned to settle at Lisieux. It was to her brother and
sister-in-law that she confided her family when she died in
1877, eleven years later.

IV

War and Unrest

UP TO THIS TIME everything was happy indeed in this family of four children, mother, father, and in-laws. Then Louis Martin's father died, the first death in the household. After this Zelie bore two sons, both of whom died soon after birth. Then came the death of her own father and of her little Helene who was five years old.

When her sister, the Visitation nun, wrote to Zelie, she said prophetically, "Your joy hereafter will be according to the measure of the consolations refused you now; for if God, accepting your sacrifice, wills to give you *this great saint whom you have so much desired for His glory,* will you not then be well repaid?"

Celine was born in 1869. Melanie Therese was born in 1870: on this occasion, too, Mrs. Martin was not able to nurse her child and had to search for a wet nurse—people in those days evidently knew little about formulas. It was breast milk or nothing. The child was neglected by the nurse and during a frantic search for a woman to take her place, the child died. Mrs. Martin mourned her as though it was her first child.

But the Franco-Prussian War was upon them and the town was about to be besieged. Half the population of seventeen thousand left, and the rest hid their valuables. Mrs. Martin wrote to her young sister-in-law: "I was not much afraid. I no longer fear anything. Had I wished to take flight, I should have come straight to you, but my husband would have been in great difficulties all alone and I, very uneasy. It was better to remain."

When the Prussians were three miles from the town, all the men were mobilized at Alençon and sent out to fight, regardless of their lack of training. "It was pitiable to see our poor soldiers return, some without feet, others without hands. I saw one whose face was all covered with blood. When there is such a shortage of men, is there any sense in sending them out to be slaughtered by such an army as we have seen? No one had any idea what the Prussian army was like; it is a very formidable war machine. There is something very sinister in the sight of their battalions, with the black flags and the death's head on their helmets. How is it that everyone does not recognize that this war is a chastisement?"

During a bombardment of the city, the family had to take refuge in the basement of their home. Afterwards, when the city was taken, twenty-five thousand marched into the town, over the Pont Neuf, passing the Martin house.

Nine soldiers were billeted with the family and of this incident she wrote:

> I am not putting myself out over them. When they demand too much I tell them that it is impossible. This morning they brought in enough meat to feed thirty people and we are now in the middle of having it cooked for them. We have been obliged to give up the entire first floor to them and to come down to the ground floor. If I told you everything I should have to write a book. The town refused to pay the sum demanded and we were threatened with reprisals. Finally, the Duke of Mecklenberg contented himself with 300,000 francs and an enormous quantity of material. All the cattle in the district have been seized. Now there is no more milk to be had anywhere. What will little Celine do, she who drank a litre a day? And how are poor mothers with infants to manage? There is no more meat in any butcher's. In short, the business of the town is stopped. Everyone is weeping except myself.

Certainly she had shed all the tears she had, it would seem, over the loss of her two infant sons, her little Helene, and now her Melanie. No material losses could bother her much. Her faith grew in her sorrow. "They are happy, and that consoles me," she wrote, "and the others, yes, the others will also enter into the heavenly kingdom, laden with more merits, since they will have fought longer." When she wrote to console her sister-in-law over the death of a little son, she said:

I am deeply grieved at the misfortune that has just struck you. Truly, you are sorely tried. It is one of your first troubles, my poor, dear sister. May our Good Lord grant you resignation to His holy will. Your dear little child is with Him. He sees you, he loves you, and you will find him again one day. This is the great comfort I feel and still feel.

When I closed the eyes of my dear children and buried them, I felt the sorrow indeed, but it has always been resigned sorrow. I did not regret the pain and cares I had borne for them. Several people said to me, "It would have been better if you had never had them," but I could not endure this sort of language. I did not think that the sufferings and anxieties could be weighed in the same scale with the eternal happiness of my children. Then they were not lost forever; life is short and full of miseries and we shall find them again up yonder. It was especially at the death of the first that I was most vividly aware of the happiness of having a child in Heaven. For God showed me in a sensible manner that He accepted my sacrifice. Through my first little angel, I obtained a very extraordinary grace.

This grace she mentioned was the sudden cure of little Helene of one of her illnesses. Helene died later at the age of five, but the grace of courage was certainly never withdrawn from her mother.

The faith of Zelie did not depend, however, on the miraculous. The illnesses and deaths in her family, the presence of the nine soldiers who were quartered with them, attention to her work which still went on, kept her from hearing much news of anything that went on outside of Alençon. Not more than seventy-five miles away, from a tiny village of eighty souls, Pontmain, the story spread that a group of children had seen an apparition of the Blessed Mother, whom the Church has since called Our Lady of Hope of Pontmain.

Two boys, ten and twelve years old, whose brother was at the front, were helping their father with his barn chores, while the mother got the supper inside the house. One of the boys stepped to the door of the barn—"I went to see what the weather was like" he said afterward, and there he saw a glorious vision of a young girl of eighteen or so, dressed in dazzling blue and white, with gold ribbons and a crown of gold, stretching her hands, palms out, towards them. His brother joining him saw the apparition also. When they called their father he saw nothing, and told them to go on with their work. But the vision was still there when they finished, and remained even after their supper. The entire village gathered, prayed the rosary, sang hymns and recited litanies. The apparition, now perceived by three other little ones from a neighboring school and two younger ones of two and six, shed the light of her smile on them, and promised them not peace but hope.

The enemy had already occupied a town a few miles away, but for no apparent reason turned back, and ten days later the peace was signed.

There was peace of a kind between the Germans and French, but there was no peace in Paris. Civil war broke out March 18, 1871, and the Archbishop of Paris and eleven priests were murdered. When the revolt was put down, after terrible reprisals, an inquiry was started, and Count de Mun, who had spent months in prison during the war, testified for the workers, saying that the blame could not be attributed to them alone. Bourgeois indifference and apathy to the conditions under which the poor lived and worked, and the terrible gulf between the classes made for class war. Industrial and city workers labored twelve hours a day or more, seven days a week. A few mild reforms in 1874 set twelve hours as a maximum for children under sixteen and forebade them night

work, but in general there were starvation wages and miserable housing. Among agricultural workers and the small hold-
ers, who made up the bulk of the population, there was a
crisis in 1876 when a disease attacked the vines and the pro-
duction of wine was cut to a third of what it had been before.

There was a growing hatred of the clergy who, in general,
aligned themselves with the monarchists, and there were only
a few enlightened Catholics who spoke out not only against
the revolution, but against the *ancien régime*.

There was terrible hardship and even starvation among the
poor, and the fear of poverty among the rich.

"I feel very well as far as bodily health is concerned,"
Zelie wrote after one terrible outbreak of rioting in Paris.
"But not in mind, especially this morning. All that is happen-
ing in Paris fills my soul with sorrow. I have just learned of
the Archbishop's death, and of the sixty-four priests shot
yesterday by the Communards. I am utterly dismayed."

When stocks went down and funds were frozen and a depression set in, she wrote, "When this tempest has passed,
we shall gather up the fragments that remain, and live on
that little."

They were thinking of the children, the four they still had
and the one who was coming. Zelie had no idea that all of
them would go into religious life, though of course there is
need for a dowry whether a girl marries or enters the convent. But whatever they possessed came from hard work,
and they always had confidence in God's providence.

Times were so bad, however, that pious folk believed the
end of the world was coming, and visions and predictions
abounded.

"I am quite decided not to take any notice of any prophet
or any prophecy. I am beginning to be very incredulous. I
say, 'God alone knows the moment and the hour.' Others
believe they see something and see nothing."

As for the prayer and penance organized in the shape of
pilgrimages, that was another matter. Louis Martin loved
travel and all his travels were a pilgrimage. Twenty thousand

made a pilgrimage to Chartres Cathedral where, it is said, before the coming of Christ, druids raised an altar to the Virgin who would bear a child.

On returning from another pilgrimage Louis Martin was jeered at and insulted, and although he bravely made his way through a demonstrating mob, some other members of the pilgrimage were arrested for taking part in an illegal procession. Mayor and councilmen attended civil funerals, and opponents of the Church were from all classes. The State in France was as officially atheist as is the U.S.S.R. now.

It is a delight to read Zelie's letters and we get to know her through them. She probably did little reading; her household work and her lacemaking must have kept her occupied, yet she found time to write constantly to her sister-in-law after her own sister died. Perhaps it was at the bedsides of the sick that she wrote. One wonders how she found the time.

One thing that struck me as most remarkable was Zelie's fearlessness. She even traveled to Le Mans to bring home her two eldest daughters, when the enemy was at the gates. There seemed to be no propaganda about Germans bayoneting babies, chopping off the hands of children, or raping women, such as we became so familiar with during the first World War. It is true the Germans did bombard the city, but when the nine German soldiers were quartered with the family, there was evidently no fear of torture, rape or other reprisals against the inhabitants of the town.

Zelie looked upon what she called the "war machine" with horror, and felt with common sense that it was futile and sinful to fight when there was so little chance of success. St. Thomas Aquinas lays down as one of his conditions for a just war that there must be some chance of success, and also that the means of conducting the war be controllable and honorable. Neither nuclear weapons, nor lying propaganda would have been acceptable means in those days.

In the midst of the aftermath of war, depression and social unrest, it is interesting to get a glimpse of the social life of the time.

You will be amused at the account of a fancy dress ball, given by Mme. Y, which has made a great stir at Alençon. Everybody is talking about it. It was magnificent, admirable, unique. Nothing has been seen like it since Alençon existed. [Zelie was quite scornful of frivolity.] Mme. Y was a queen and had a gold crown with a veil spangled with stars. Mme. O was a Folly. She wore a dress of yellow muslin which was so tight as to make her utterly ridiculous. When she appeared in this get-up and saw how rich were the dresses of the other ladies, she did not know where to hide herself. I learnt all these details from persons who were present at the notorious ball, which ended at five o'clock in the morning. As a finale they had a grand dinner, after which all the guests went to bed.

It was necessary to strengthen the floor of the ball room with props; otherwise the dancers would have fallen into the room beneath. I forgot to mention that these rooms were decorated with garlands of flowers and trails of ivy. It is a pity to go to so much trouble and expense to be made a laughing stock.

Another letter she wrote showed an incident in the bitter class war of the time.

A curious adventure took place recently in connection with a lady whose barouche was standing opposite to our house, outside the Prefecture. The coachman wore gorgeous livery lavishly trimmed with fur. A discontented individual carrying a canvas sack in his hand was just passing by. He stopped for a moment to survey the coachman and then the lady inside the carriage. Then he turned to the open door, undid his bag and threw the contents into her lap.

At once, she cried out in terror. The coachman came to her assistance, the passers-by ran up. There they saw her convulsed in a nervous attack, and swarming over her were about twenty frogs. They were even on her head; in fact she was covered with them.

The wretched assailant watched her struggling when the policeman arrived on the scene and asked him why he had done such a thing. He quietly replied, "I had just caught these frogs to sell, but when I saw this aristocrat, with her coachman all decked out in furs, I preferred to give her a good fright rather than sell my frogs." They took him to the gaol; he did not try to escape.

The Martins may have accepted the class system and recognized those whom the society of the day called the great ladies. But Zelie and Louis did not esteem such people. However, Zelie's charity was such that what scorn she showed was a gentle one. And her love for the poor was genuine. The Martins themselves did more than tithe; they administered to the poor, gave one day a week to their calls, and taught their children that it was a privilege to serve the unfortunate with their own hands and do the works of mercy directly instead of doling out advice and pious admonitions. Louis Martin was a pioneer in the Workmen's Circles, the groups started in France by Count Albert de Mun and René de la Tour du Pin as a result of their study of the thought of Bishop von Ketteler and that of the papal encyclicals on the Church, the State and liberty.

In spite of war and disorder, the work necessary to sustain life went on, and the Martins soon discovered that there was not room for two businesses under one roof. There had been room for fathers-in-law and for all the children God chose to send and for the quartering of soldiers, but two businesses were too much. Zelie Martin had given up her lacemaking for a time, but then they moved to another house, and it was then that Mr. Martin retired from his watchmaking and entered into partnership with his wife in lacemaking.

She had the usual changeable attitude toward work. Sometimes she loved it. At other times: "This lace will be the death of me!" At the latter time she was plagued with a great number of orders which had to be finished in spite of sickness in the home.

But there was a living to earn now for a household consisting of five children, a servant, and the parents. There was also provision to be made for the children in the future. Who could tell what their needs would be? Who could tell what would happen in the future, what wars between nations or between classes would wipe out this or that aspect of their security? They had their hands and their strength, and as long as these endured, the Martins would work. They would save, as they had in the past, and their saving would make the kind of a home where it would be easier to be good. Zelie had saved as a girl; undoubtedly she had helped to launch her brother in his business, sent aid to her sister at the convent, and contributed to foreign missions. Certainly the overflow of a life of hard work is often a rich one. It was a life of pilgrimages, holidays, small comforts, but never self-indulgence, never luxury.

St. Thomas Aquinas said that a certain amount of goods are necessary to lead a good life. And Peter Maurin, the peasant, said that our aim, if we love our brothers, is to make that kind of a society where it is easier for people to be good. The Martins well knew that the beginnings of peace, the beginnings of a good society are in the home; if it has ever been easy to be good, it was in that little home in a small town in France which perhaps would never have been heard from had not one of the daughters turned out to be a saint.

V

Therese is Born

THERESE WAS BORN of a love match. One might say that Zelie had fallen in love with Louis Martin when she first saw him, at that slight meeting when they passed each other on the Pont Neuf. She had wanted to get married, it is true. She had chosen the convent first and when she was refused at the convent of her choice, she immediately accepted that refusal as the voice of God for her. That acceptance in itself was a great grace. There seemed to be no uncertainty in her mind, no wondering whether she should try this convent or that, whether God wanted her perhaps in another convent. When she was rejected she did not allow a sense of "rejection," that grief which the world of psychiatry talks so much about these days, to sadden her. She started out to earn a living, to learn a skill to earn a living. If she had lived today, she might have gone into a factory or an office. But she chose to learn lace-making, a work that could be done in the home, and was not calculated to bring her much into contact with men. She wanted to get married, but she did not seem unduly concerned with it. She applied herself to her craft which she evidently enjoyed, devoted herself to her charitable work, as well as to Church services, and waited. Marriage came to her in God's good time.

One letter will serve to show the feeling she had for her husband. It was written on the occasion of a visit to her brother. Unlike her husband, who loved traveling, she made much of a small expedition. She wrote in August, 1873:

My dear Louis,

We arrived yesterday afternoon at half-past four; my brother met us at the station and was delighted to see us. Both he and his wife are doing everything to entertain us.

This evening, Sunday, there is a pleasant party in our honor. Tomorrow, Monday, we are going to Trouville. Tuesday, there is to be a big dinner at the house of Mme. Maudelonde and perhaps a drive to the country house of Mme. Fournet. The children are in raptures, and their happiness will be complete if the weather is fine.

But for myself, I find it hard to relax. Nothing of that interests me! I feel just like the fish you take out of the water; they are no longer in their element and must perish.

This would have the same effect on me if my stay had to be very prolonged. I feel ill at ease. I am not in my niche, and that overflows into the physical sphere and I feel almost ill. However, I reason with myself and try to master the feeling. I am with you all day in spirit, and say to myself: "Now he is doing such and such a thing."

I long to be with you, Louis dear. I love you with all my heart and I feel my affection doubled by being deprived of your company. I could not live apart from you.

This morning I heard three Masses. I went to the six o'clock, made my thanksgiving and said my prayers during the seven, and came back for the High Mass.

My brother is not displeased over business. He is doing quite well.

Tell Leonie and Celine that I send my love and kiss them both, and that I will bring them a keepsake from Lisieux.

If possible I will try and write tomorrow, but I do not know what time we shall return from Trouville. I am in a hurry for they are waiting for me to go visiting. We shall arrive home on Wednesday evening at half past seven. How long it seems till then!

I embrace you as I love you. The little girls wish me to tell you they are enjoying themselves at Lisieux and send you a big hug.

A letter from Louis, dated ten years earlier, shows the same love and regard.

Dearest,

I cannot arrive at Alencon before Monday. The time passes slowly for I long to be with you. I need not say I was very pleased to receive your letter, except that I see by it that you are overtiring yourself. So I recommend calm and moderation, above all in your lace work. I have some orders from the Compagnie Lyonnaise. Once more, do not worry so much. With God's help we shall manage to keep up a nice little home.

I had the happiness to communicate at Our Lady of Victories, which is like a little heaven on earth. I put up a candle for all the family intentions.

I kiss you all lovingly, whilst awaiting the pleasure of being with you again. I hope Marie and Pauline are being very good!

Your husband and true friend who loves you forever.

Years later, Pauline was to say in testifying in the process of beatification, "My parents always seemed to me to be saints. We were filled with respect and admiration for them. Sometimes I asked myself if there could be others like them on earth. I never saw any such around me."

Zelie was over forty and her husband nearly fifty when Therese, the ninth child, was born, January 2, 1873. On the day of her birth, a poor child of a family which the Martins were helping came to the door with a paper bearing the following verse:

> Smile and swiftly grow;
> All beckons thee to joy,
> Sweet love and tenderest care.
> Smile gladly at the dawn,
> Which only lasts an hour!
> For thou shalt grow to be
> A stately rose.

On January 4 she was baptized in the Church of Notre

Dame with her elder sister Marie as her godmother. She was given, as all the other children had been, the name Marie, to which Françoise-Therese was added. The Francoise was for St. Francis de Sales, in consideration for Zelie's sister, the nun in the Visitation Order which was founded by that saint.

Zelie's eighth child also had been baptized Therese; she wrote to her sister-in-law that she would never get over this little girl's death, that indeed she never expected to have another child. And yet here was another little Therese, baptized a child of God and an heir of heaven, and destined to be the greatest saint of our times.

"I was born to have children," Zelie said joyfully. "I am madly fond of them." And she said that while she was carrying Therese something happened which had never happened with her others. "When I am singing, she sings with me. I tell it to you in confidence. No one would believe it."

"She smiles already," her mother wrote a few days after Therese's birth. "She looked at me attentively, and then gave me a delightful smile."

But Zelie, though she tried desperately, was not able to nurse this little one either. Within a few weeks the child had intestinal trouble, and the mother could not sleep nights for worrying. With the prayers of her aunt at the Visitation Convent, the baby grew better for a while but in March she became worse. The doctor's opinion was that only breast feeding could save her and Zelie thought of a wet nurse she had employed before, "Little Rose." All one night she waited for dawn to go on her errand. Her husband was away on business, and she could not entrust the task to anyone else.

"The night seemed long," she wrote. "All the gravest symptoms which preceded the deaths of my other little ones were showing themselves and I was very sad. I set off at daybreak for the nurse, who lives at Semallé, about six miles from Alencon. On the lonely road I met two men who rather frightened me, but I said to myself, 'I should not care if they killed me!' I felt death in my soul."

She had a hard time persuading the good peasant woman,

Rose, to go at once to the Martin home. Her husband did
not want her to leave. After all they had four children of their
own, the youngest a year old! It was wonderful that she still
had milk in her breasts. There was the work of the little
farm, the cow which was called Redskin, and the little white
farmhouse. Even after Rose consented to go with Zelie and
had set out on the road, the husband sent one of the other
children after her ordering her to return home. But she went
on, and when she got to the Martin house and saw the condition of the baby, she did not hold out much hope for the
life of the child.

Zelie was so overcome by fatigue and grief that she hastened to her room and knelt down for a moment before a
statue of St. Joseph, foster-father of the Infant Jesus, who certainly must have worried in his life over the condition of the
Child born in winter in a cave, warmed only by the heat of a
few animals around Him. While Zelie prayed for the life of
Therese, she kept saying at the same time, "God's will be
done."

When she went downstairs she found the child feeding
greedily. Suddenly, according to the mother's letter, she
ceased and relinquished the breast and suddenly fell like one
dead.

There were five of us around her. All were shocked. One
of my laceworkers was there crying and I felt my blood
freeze. The baby did not seem to be breathing. We bent
over her, trying in vain to find a sign of life. We saw none,
but she was so quiet and peaceful that I thanked God she
had died so easily. At last, after a quarter of an hour, my
Therese opened her eyes and began to smile. From that
moment she was completely cured. Her healthy look returned, as also her liveliness. Since then, all is as well as
could be.

But my baby has gone away. It is very sad to have
brought up a child for two months and then be compelled
to entrust her to the care of strangers.

The husband of Rose had insisted on his wife's return, so

the child went to the home of the peasants and lived with them for over a year. It was a true peasant's hut, made of stone and mud with a thatched roof, with a manure pile in the yard next door. The baby had another attack at the end of March, but then warm weather came and life in the open air. Zelie wrote, "She is sunburnt. Her nurse wheels her in the fields, perched on top of bundles of grass in a wheelbarrow. She carries her in her apron when she goes to milk the cow and even ties her on the back of the cow to leave her arms free."

The baby was never content save with her nurse. If Rose went to Mass, leaving the infant at the Martin home, the child screamed until someone went to the church to fetch her. When Rose went to market day in the town, Therese had to be taken too, and a place found for her at the stall where butter and eggs were sold. She went to the arms of the other lacemakers when brought to the Martin house for a visit, but anyone in fine dress she rejected, her mother said. She liked the smell of the poor!

"My little Therese has been walking alone since Thursday. She is as sweet and good as an angel and has delightful ways, and such a sweet smile. I long to have her home."

It was not until April when the baby was fifteen months old that she returned home to her parents. Then she followed her mother about everywhere, clinging to her as she sat at her work, pleasing her by her devotion, and yet "an inconvenience sometimes." It must have been hard to get work done, with a fifteen-month-old child among the needles and pins of lacemaking. Mr. Martin put up a swing for her in the little garden when she was eighteen months old and she loved that, demanding to be swung high. She had the usual imperious airs of much-loved children.

The parents delighted in her. But neither their work nor their children kept them from getting to daily Mass, and every morning at six found them in the neighboring church.

VI

Zelie Dies

AND NOW THERE is the story of Zelie's terrible last illness. She had written to her sister-in-law that her health was good, but all the while death was at her breast.

The lump that appeared there was first noticed in 1865. Nothing was done about it. It was not the habit of the day to perform an operation (a slight one) to remove the danger. Ten years later the swelling became greatly enlarged and painful, sometimes with a continual dull ache, and other times with fierce shooting pains. Then a numbness set in through her side. When she consulted a doctor he held out no hope. He was a good doctor, but one without faith. He evidently did not have much of the famed bedside manner, or was it that he wanted to try her faith? He did not hesitate to tell her that there was no hope for her. "He has rendered me one service," she wrote her sister-in-law. "That consultation was priceless to me."

> I could not help telling them everything at home. I am sorry now for it was a heart-rending scene. Everyone cried; Poor Leonie sobbed. But I told them of how many people had lived in this state for ten or fifteen years, and I seemed so little upset, doing my ordinary work as cheerfully as usually, perhaps more so, that I calmed them a little.
> However I am very far from being under any illusions and I can scarcely sleep at night when I think of the future.

All the same I am doing my best to be resigned, though I was far from expecting such a trial.

My husband is inconsolable. He has lost his pleasure in fishing, put away his rods in the attic, and no longer cares to go to the Club. He is as though completely crushed. . . .

I am very anxious that this should not sadden you too much and that you should be resigned to the will of God. If He thought that I was very necessary to this earth, certainly He would not allow me to have this disease, for I have so often prayed that He might not take me from this world so long as I was necessary to my children.

Marie is now grown up; her character is of a very serious cast and she has none of the illusions of youth. I am sure that when I am no longer here she will make a good mistress of the home, and do her utmost to bring up her little sisters and set a good example. Pauline also is charming, but Marie has more experience. Besides, she has much authority over her little sisters. Celine has an excellent disposition and is a very pious child; it is rare to see a child of her age show such inclinations to religion. Therese is really a little angel. As for Leonie, only God Himself can change her, and I have the conviction that He will. . . .

They will be very fortunate in having you when I shall be no longer here. You will help them with your good advice and should they have the misfortune to lose their father, you would take them to your home, would you not?

It comforts me much to think that I have good relations who will replace me advantageously in case of need. There are poor mothers far more unhappily situated than I, who do not know what is to become of their children, who leave them in need without any assistance. I have nothing to fear on that score. In short, I do not see things through dark glasses. It is a great grace which God is giving me.

Certainly not many people can so contemplate their end, so prepare for it, and think of a lingering and painful death as a grace.

When, to satisfy her relatives, Zelie consulted a famous surgeon of the day at Lisieux she wrote her husband, "The doctor considers it very regrettable that the operation was not performed at the very first, but it is now too late. However, he seemed to think that I can go on for a very long time like this. So let us leave it all in God's hands. He knows what is for our good much better than we do. It is He Who wounds, and He Who heals. I will go to Lourdes on the first pilgrimage, and I hope that our Lady will cure me if that be necessary. In the meantime let us be tranquil. I am rejoicing much at the thought of seeing you all again. How long the time seems. How I should have liked to return today. I am only happy when I am with you, Louis dear."

After this consultation, life continued as before in the Martin home, and Zelie discouraged any talking about her illness. She fasted and abstained on the appointed days, and did not leave any religious duties or any of her housework undone. Letters show that the family life continued to be lively during the recreations, the feast days. The family attended a fair, they made fritters for a feast day and carnival. "She humorously laid the blame for her trouble on Adam and Eve."

She thought at first of giving up her business, but there were orders she felt had to be carried out, and because some people who were trying to buy the business turned out to be dishonest, she continued her work to the end. "I feel I need rest," she wrote, "but I shall hardly have any before that which is eternal."

As the disease progressed and the pain increased and other swellings appeared in the neck she wrote again to her sister-in-law. "God is granting me the grace not to feel frightened. I am very peaceful. I feel almost happy. I would not change my lot for any other whatsoever. If God wills to cure me, I shall be very glad in my heart, I want to live. It costs me much to leave my husband and children. But on the other hand, I feel myself that if I am not cured it will be because it is more expedient for them that I go. I have hardly cause to rejoice at seeing the time drawing nearer, but I am like children who do not worry over the morrow."

Zelie had always so loved her sister that she called her the soul of her soul. She also loved the other Visitation nuns, even though they had refused to keep Leonie, who was not a good pupil and who was too difficult for the nuns to manage. Now that Zelie knew she was going to die, she went to pay a last visit to her beloved sister, who had been suffering from tuberculosis for the past two years and was not herself expected to live much longer. Out of consideration for Sister Marie Dosithea's illness, Zelie did not speak of her own.

When she visited the convent at Le Mans, she could also see her favorite child, Pauline, who was still going to school, though Marie was now at home. It was the last time Zelie saw her sister, who died a month later, in February, 1877.

In June Mrs. Martin set out on a pilgrimage with Leonie and Marie, stopping at Le Mans to pick up Pauline, stopping again at Angers to visit the shrine of St. Margaret Mary, and then proceeding to Lourdes, that little mountain village close to the southern border of France, a long train ride for an invalid. It was a hard trip and it was in a state of utter exhaustion that Zelie arrived there in time to go directly to Mass, and then to the baths. Traveling was difficult for her always; she always made too much trouble of it. She never liked being away from home even on a trip to see her brother and sister-in-law and to rest and be entertained. This last trip was an agony. She fell and twisted her neck so that the resulting pain never ceased until her death. They had a hard time finding lodgings in the crowded little town, and the food was bad. On the train some of the pilgrims had tried to make coffee over an alcohol lamp and it had overturned and spilled water over their clothes. She could still suffer from these little things, she who so loved to dress her daughters. And the girls suffered on seeing their mother suffer.

She stayed to be immersed in the baths half a dozen times but to no avail. They hoped for a miracle, but there was no miracle and the girls were even more bitterly disappointed than she was. Her pains were eased by submersion in the icy water, but as soon as she left the baths, the pains returned.

One great joy Zelie Martin had on this trip was to meet a

woman who had been daily with Bernadette and could tell of the tremendous beauty which shone from the face of the peasant child when she knelt in ecstasy in the disordered dumping ground where she had gone with her companions to gather wood, and had instead seen a miraculous vision of the Blessed Virgin. Bernadette's face had been so transformed by love and light, a reflection of the beauty of heaven, that those who had seen her could never forget it.

It is said that when cures are not effected at Lourdes there is instead a great grace given—courage, strength, and peace to accept pain and death.

It was in a most cheerful mood that Zelie returned to Alençon, chiding her daughters for their disappointment. It was good to be home with the other two little ones, and to enjoy them to the full for the few remaining months of her life. She continued to get to Mass early in the morning. She knelt always to say the rosary in her room.

The pain began to be terrible in July when she wrote to her brother. She could not sleep for more than a few moments at a time. There was no position where she could be at ease. No remedies seemed to help. Often Marie, Louis, and the nursing sister who came now to help, all tried to make her comfortable, to sit up with her. But she preferred to be alone, knowing that nothing could help her and not wishing to disturb them. Marie could hear her at night pleading, "Oh, Thou Who hast made me, have mercy on me." But when she went in to her mother, there was nothing she could do and Zelie chided her for getting up.

On August 3, the first Friday of the month, she dragged herself to church for the last time. From then on she had to keep to her room.

How hard she tried to keep up! Marie was giving the two little ones, Celine and Therese, their lessons every day, and on August 9 they had a little party and prizegiving, which was held in the mother's room. Then again on the feast of St. Louis, August 24, 1877, which they had always tried to celebrate in honor of the father, whose name day it was, there was another party. On the next day Zelie was anointed and all the children knelt about her bed as she received the last rites of the Church.

The priest's first long prayer after he sprinkles the room and those in it with holy water is:

> Along with our lowly coming, O Lord Jesus Christ, let there enter into this home unending happiness, divine blessing, untroubled joy, charity which is fruitful, continual health. Drive forth from this place the spirit of evil. Let Thine angel of peace come hither, and banish all harmful dissension from this house. O Lord, extol Thy holy Name in our esteem, and bless what we are about to do. Sanctify the coming of Thine unworthy servant, for Thou art holy, Thou art kind, Thou art abiding with the Father, and the Holy Spirit through all eternity.

> Let us pray to our Lord Jesus Christ and beseech Him to bless with His abundant benediction this home and all who dwell therein. May He appoint over them a good angel as a guardian, and assist them to serve Him, to contemplate the grandeur of His law. May He turn away all powers that would harm them, free them from all anxiety and distress, and keep them in well-being within their home, Who livest and reignest with the Father and the Holy Spirit, God, for all eternity.

> Hear us, O holy Lord, Father Almighty, eternal God. And deign to send Thy holy angel from heaven to guard, cherish, protect, abide with, and defend all who dwell in this house, through Christ our Lord.

After the priest has finished this prayer, he lays his hands on the sufferer and prays that all the power of the devil may become extinct in her, through Mary, St. Joseph, all the angels, archangels, patriarchs, prophets, apostles, martyrs, confessors, virgins, and all the other saints.

Then he anoints the eyes, ears, nose, mouth, hands and feet, begging that through this anointing whatever sins have been committed through the senses may be forgiven.

The very last prayer for the dying is of incomparable dignity:

Go forth, O Christian soul out of this world, in the name of God the Father Who created thee; in the name of Jesus Christ the Son of the living God, Who suffered for thee; in the name of the Holy Spirit Who was poured forth upon thee; in the name of the glorious and ever blessed Virgin Mary, Mother of God; in the name of Joseph, chaste spouse of the same Virgin; in the name of the angels and archangels, in the names of the thrones and dominations; in the name of the principalities and powers; in the name of the cherubim and seraphim; in the name of the patriarchs and prophets; in the name of the holy apostles and evangelists; in the name of the holy martyrs and confessors; in the name of the holy monks and hermits; in the name of the holy virgins and all the saints of God, may thy place be this day in peace, and thine abode in holy Sion. Through Christ, our Lord, Amen.

Zelie died on August 27, a little after midnight. Leonie, Pauline, and Marie were called to her bedside, but the two little girls were not awakened.

She was buried Wednesday, August 29, after a nine o'clock requiem Mass, leaving five daughters: Marie, seventeen and a half; Pauline, sixteen; Leonie, fifteen; Celine, eight; and Therese, four and a half.

VII

The Sisters of the Little Flower

WHAT WERE THESE sisters like? Marie was the oldest, and we get a picture of her from the biography which is usually written when a Carmelite sister dies and the obituary is sent around the world to the other Carmels. Pauline, the second sister, wrote the life of Marie, who died at the age of eighty after spending fifty-three years and three months in a Carmelite convent. Pauline was Mother Superior of the convent after the death of Mother de Gonzague, and so was in a position to ask Marie for material for the little biography which she was to write later.

"Marie's brief notes and letters, written to me at my express command," according to Pauline, "will give a clear understanding of my dear sister during her earliest years." (Marie disliked setting forth her thoughts and it was only under obedience to her sister that she would write.)

"Marie was very independent and the first notable instance of this occurred when Louise, our very officious maid, who always had her own way with the younger girls, so that they never dared oppose her, attempted to bring Marie under her rigorous surveillance. But her commands were issued in too sharp a manner to suit Marie, who would fearlessly reply, 'Let me alone, Louise! I am quite free.' Hence the maid nicknamed her, 'I-am-quite-free.' "

Marie herself wrote:

> When I was brought to church and heard the little bell
> at the moment of elevation, seeing everyone bow their
> heads, I would say to myself: "What a pity we have to bow
> our heads! I prefer to watch—I am quite free." And as a
> matter of fact, that is just what I did. I can still see the
> white Host in the hands of the priest. Later, when I under-
> stood why all heads were bowed, I continued to contem-
> plate the Sacred Host, now not independently but devoutly.
>
> Moreover, I did not like to bow to persons of our ac-
> quaintance. It humiliated me to bow. I remember one day
> on the way to our summer house, such an occasion pre-
> sented itself and I turned my head away like a little savage.
> Mother was greatly pained to discover so eccentric a trait
> in me and she told me I should never be loved. But this
> only helped to strengthen me in my pride. Convinced that
> politeness and bowing were necessary before others would
> love me, I said to myself, "It is decidedly unpleasant to try
> to make others love me. No, I'll not so demean myself!"
> And I said to my mother, "I don't care if other people do
> not love me. If you love me that is enough."

She was eight and a half when she was sent away to the
boarding school of the Visitation convent at Le Mans where
her aunt was a nun, and despite the fact that she had her sister Pauline, who was seven, with her, Marie suffered terribly
at being separated from her parents. When they came to see
her, she clung to their hands, and when walking with them
would not release them even to pick flowers, which she
wanted very much. She spent seven years at Le Mans, aside
from holidays at home, and never got used to the separation.
During the year when the Little Flower was boarded out in
the country, Marie was sent home from school with a fever,
which was supposed to be typhoid. She was thirteen then.
According to Pauline, the doctor said to her parents, "This
fever is due to a nervous condition, rather than to typhus.
She must have been upset in some way." The young invalid
heard and was "comforted to think now there was proof of
what she had suffered at the separation from her parents."

When Marie recovered, Zelie suggested that she give up her studies at Le Mans and continue them at Alencon, but the child had great affection for her aunt and did not want to hurt her.

Although she loved her aunt, she criticized her, too. "When I was about eleven or twelve I was often a source of annoyance to my aunt who had till then been so pleased with me. For example, I once said to her, in all sincerity, 'Aunt, I find that there are many words repeated in the Gospel but our rhetoric teacher tells us to avoid repetition.' She took on a severe and almost indignant air, and said to me, 'Are you trying to improve on the words of our Lord?' I who was only confiding in her, was taken aback by the very idea, and said to myself: 'Very well, I'll not attempt to reveal such ideas to her again, since she makes so much ado about it.' "

When she returned to school she met a new student, a young girl her own age to whom she was much drawn, and the two became fast friends. The other was rich and noble and beautiful besides, and Marie lost her freedom of heart for a while. She took on airs and graces and was proud of being a student at the Visitation Convent, where most of the pupils belonged to the nobility and had estates. One time when she was walking with her father and had picked a bouquet which she said she was bringing back to school after her holiday in memory of their little country place, her father teased her and said, "and you will probably call it your estate." The girl flung her bouquet away and was provoked that her motives were so evident.

This phase evidently lasted some little time, because even after she left school at fifteen and started to help her mother run the house and sew, she was always hankering for a bigger house and wishing that they lived somewhere else. She disdained "piety" and this distressed her mother, who persuaded her to make a retreat. She was just as indifferent when she returned home after her week, and it was not until she had made two more retreats that she found herself, as it were, and went through something like a conversion.

She attended dances and social functions with the approval of her mother, who dressed her with pride, and impatiently put aside the objections of her holy sister the nun, who wanted her nieces to have no part in the world.

Though she went to social functions, she hated being dressed up or made up. When her mother wanted her to wear a medallion around her neck or a velvet ribbon, she said she felt like a poodle dog. She hated little half-veils and once when some clothes were being tried on, she rushed from the house weeping, declaring that they were trying to marry her off. She sounds very much like a typical adolescent and when we consider her later care of her little sister and the efficiency with which she ran her father's house, she seems to have got through this period quickly and safely.

Eleven years after meeting her friend at school, whose name has not come down to us, Marie saw her again for a last time, just before she herself entered Carmel. Before, when they had been at school, it was this girl who had cherished dreams of a convent life. Now her course had taken a different turn. Marie had written of this period, which Pauline did not hesitate to call her "inordinate attachment," "Alas, instead of entertaining foolish dreams of creatures, would I have flown straight to You, O my God, like my little Therese. For You also dream of creatures . . . but You do not dream as we do. . . . You dream of the creature in order to deify it, and sometimes—O Mystery—You dream of it to make it Your spouse! And this is the dream of love that has been realized in me."

At that last meeting Marie said of her friend "All her beauty had withered like the flower of the field. For myself, I hastened to fly toward the unique Beauty, Beauty which never fades. My dreams of nobility and grandeur had passed."

Pauline hastens to tell us, in the very next paragraph, that "Marie was tall and beautiful, pure as a lily with a purity she would never soil." They both speak of the attachment as being "inordinate," but Marie's pride and the holiness of their surroundings kept this young love from being the murky, perverse passion which it might under other circumstances have become, and sometimes does become in girls' schools.

The aunt advised her to say daily the prayer beginning, "O St. Joseph, Father and Protector of Virgins," Pauline goes on. But when Marie saw written on the leaflet, "special prayer for priests and religious," she said: "So! My aunt wants me to be a religious. There is no danger that I'll say that prayer!"

She evidently loved taking care of children, and tutored Celine and afterward Therese, and always Leonie, who had been sent home twice from the Visitation school at Le Mans and went to day school in Alencon to the Benedictines.

When her mother and her aunt indulged in what she called "pious exhortations" which she herself said never "had much effect on her," she said to her mother, "Mama, I do assure you that I love the good God very much, even more than you think. Thus, I love to look at the tabernacle. It is not worth the trouble moving my lips. I simply prefer to hide my feelings."

Her aunt asked her to go to her retreat master to discuss her vocation. In order to satisfy Sister Dosithea, she said to the priest that she was coming to him to discover her vocation; would he please reveal it to her so that there could be no further question about it? Was this a sense of humor on her part, or was she one of those direct souls that live from day to day untroubled by the future?

"I did not think of my vocation," she confided later. "I had none. I did the best I could. I asked this good religious to take me under his direction. He gave me his address. I was sincere, yet quite determined never to write to him. Behold the result of this retreat."

And yet her mother wrote to her sister, "I am quite satisfied with Marie. The things of this world do not penetrate her heart as deeply as do spiritual things. She is becoming very pious. I think that she will be a religious. I would like her to be a saint."

Marie was almost twenty-six years old when she went to Carmel. Her going was more in the spirit of the older St.

Teresa of Avila than of the young St. Therese who was to come after her. Witty and sometimes brusque in speech, Marie was fiercely independent: "I wish to be free." She did not feel that marriage was her vocation, but she was repelled by the idea of being "an old maid." However, she wanted a sign. It was the Jesuit, Reverend Father Pichon, who "caught her in the net of kindness" and by a few direct queries, by asking her to write down her impressions of the religious life, settled her vocation. She had left him with her heart filled with a secret joy, she said, feeling that she had been chosen, and that "she would not be like the young man who turned away from our Lord, after Jesus had said, 'Come, follow Me.'"

Her father seemed deeply saddened by her decision. He had thought that she would be with him always, and said so. She was his first born, and she was a good companion besides. But he placed no obstacles in her path when she announced her decision. By now Celine, seventeen, was old enough to manage the household. Therese was fourteen then and Leonie twenty-three. They did not count much on Leonie's stability.

Marie's first impressions of the convent were not at all reassuring. She thought it very bare and poor, shut in and meager compared to the spacious grounds of the Visitation Convent where she had lived for seven years. But, she said, she was, after all, quite accustomed to life behind bars.

Her aunt and uncle, according to her own account, were astonished that she who had always the air of not being able to endure convents was going to be a nun. "I, the independent one!" she adds.

Marie was the oldest, but she was the second to leave home. Pauline had left them when she was twenty-one years old, and there had never seemed to be any problem about her vocation or as to whether or not she was devout. She was short, dark and slight in appearance; her personality was aloof and she had the manner of one born to command respect, born to govern. Marie was perhaps warmer, simpler, less gifted. But it would be hard to judge this from reading Marie's letters and her detailed biography, which was written partly by her and partly by Pauline. Both sisters were unusual. It is interesting to see the differences in their handwriting. Pauline's is rather bold and direct. Marie's is smaller, more regular, and has less dash. Marie used to call herself a blockhead when it came to discussing controversial issues and she confessed she did not care much about learned books. She wanted the "little way" of her sister; she wanted to go straight to God. It is to Marie that Therese afterwards addresses her last chapter on the way of spiritual childhood.

There had never been any problems in relation to Marie and Pauline. Marie was her father's favorite child, his diamond, as he called her, Pauline was her mother's. Zelie confessed to her sister that in her prayers she had described to the Blessed Mother just the kind of child she would like, "dotting the i's and crossing the t's." And she claimed that in Pauline she got just what she wanted. There was no rivalry, no jealousy between the two sisters. They loved each other dearly and were inseparable. The mother confided in Pauline as to a friend, and looked to her with joy and love, almost as a leader among the others. She knew this daughter would be a nun, and it was something that mother and daughter accepted long before Zelie's death.

But Leonie, the third daughter, was always the problem child. Little is said about this by the other sisters. Never does Therese comment on it. There is no mention of it in the autobiography of the Little Flower. Celine speaks merely of Leonie as being "moody." But Leonie herself spoke later of her "detestable childhood."

She was sickly as a baby and seemed to have a chronic whooping cough. She was slow in walking and there was a running eczema over her whole body. Till the age of sixteen months, according to her mother, she hovered between life and death, and Louis Martin made a pilgrimage on foot to a shrine of our Lady for her cure. Leonie recovered finally at the end of a novena to St. Margaret Mary, the Visitation nun who brought renewed devotion to the Sacred Heart. This is one of those particular devotions so familiar to Catholics, but one that is of prime importance since it emphasizes the humanity of Christ and the love of His human as well as divine heart for all men.

Later on Zelie writes about her unruly child to her sister. Why, she queries, did God heal her daughter if He did not intend to listen to her prayers now for her reform?

In this day it is often the difficult child that is sent away to a school, rather than the oldest and brightest and most useful members of the family. Leonie by her own words was so backward that she still had to be tutored at the age of twenty-three. She said she had always suffered from a sense of her inferiority. On those occasions when Leonie, too, was sent away to the Visitation convent at Le Mans, she was so difficult that the Sisters had to send her home. She was described as too capricious and too backward. But her aunt had confidence that one day "she would be as good as her sisters."

Leonie was first sent home by the Visitation nuns in 1872, when she was nine. In January, 1875, the mother tried again, sending her to the convent to be prepared for first Holy Communion. Corrections and reproofs had no effect on her; unremitting kindness was tried and at first this worked out well, but soon the child again became unmanageable. Once more, in April of the same year, she was sent home again because of inattention and unruly behavior.

There was another incident in the life of Leonie which showed how hard pressed her mother was for time to care for her, what with the care of dying infants, in-laws, and her work in her own home. It showed too, how difficult a child Leonie was, that there was always this attempt made to find another place for her, since the convent for well-bred little girls would not take her. In Alençon there were two school-teachers who wore religious garb and evidently provided a foster-home for a few children. There Leonie was sent—we do not know whether she was boarded there or whether she was sent by the day. It was there that Mrs. Martin found that the two women were cruelly treating a little girl of eight, starving her and "exploiting" her, which meant, I suppose, that they were overworking her. Mrs. Martin fed the child secretly, and intervened with the mother and with the parish priest and, getting no satisfaction in either case, had to go to the local magistrate. The child, dragged into court and terrorized, denied any starvation and cruelty, and there was quite a public stir over the matter, which must have been very painful to the home-loving Zelie, who could only have forced the issue in this way because she was convinced of her facts. Although the superintendent of police of Alençon was on her side, Zelie was able to accomplish little to remedy the situation, even when she offered to pay for the child's board at a refuge. She wrote to Pauline and told her the story, and told her too that she had to develop a "sort of protective armor around her sensitiveness," to keep from being hurt at these failures.

There was nothing sentimental about Zelie's charity. She worked at her own problems as best she could, by trial and error, the way most of us do, and if she made a mistake in sending her difficult child into such a situation, she was able to do something, perhaps, for the miserable little victim of man's cruelty she encountered there. It was, too, another step in Leonie's development, one which made her without doubt more tender toward the poor.

Zelie wrote to her sister-in-law about how upset she was. If a child was difficult, then it was up to the parents to do something about it. She had sent Leonie to Le Mans because of her confidence in her sister. "My one hope of reforming this child lay in my sister, and I was persuaded that they would keep her. But despite the best will in the world, it was necessary to separate her from the other children. As soon as she is with companions, she seems to lose control of herself, and you never saw anything like her unruliness. Well, I have no longer any hope of changing her nature save by a miracle. It is true that I do not deserve a miracle but I am hoping

against all hope. The more difficult she seems, the more I am
persuaded that God will not let her remain like this."

It was not until March, 1877, the year of Zelie's death,
when Leonie was fourteen years old, that a change occurred.

Zelie's sister had died in January, still reassuring her sister
about her difficult child, insisting that some day she would be
a Visitation nun. In March Zelie wrote to her confidante,
Pauline:

> I believe I have obtained a great grace through your
> aunt's prayers. . . .
>
> You know what your sister was like; a model of insub-
> ordination, having never obeyed me save when forced to
> do so. In a spirit of contradiction she would do precisely
> the contrary of what I wished, even when she would have
> wished to do the thing asked of her. In short she obeyed
> only the maid.
>
> I had tried by every means in my power to win her.
> Everything had failed up to this day, and it was the great-
> est sorrow I have ever had in my life. Since your aunt died,
> I have implored her to win the heart of this child for me,
> and on Sunday morning I was heard. I now have it as com-
> pletely as I could have wished. She will no longer leave me
> for a moment, kisses me until she nearly stifles me, does
> anything I bid her without question, and works beside me
> all the day long.
>
> The maid has entirely lost her authority and it is certain
> that she will never again have any ascendancy over Leonie
> after the manner in which things have turned out. She, the
> servant, wept and moaned when I told her to leave imme-
> diately, but I no longer wished to have her in my sight.
> She has so besought me to let her remain that I am going
> to wait a little, but she is forbidden to address a word to
> Leonie. I am now treating the child so gently that, little by
> little, I hope to succeed in correcting her faults.

The mystery was this. Louise, the maid who had been with
them so many years and seemed so devoted to the family,
had decided to take a hand with the difficult and moody child
and through a system of terrorism she had exacted obedience.

"She made use of her domineering manner," Father Piat says, and terrified Leonie, who "became her slave, beaten and content to be so." Under her influence Leonie obeyed no one but her, and had become a "hypocrite and a rebel."

Marie who was now home from school and who shared the responsibility of teaching and caring for Leonie, had overheard a conversation that enabled her to win the child's confidence. As a result, Marie was able to discover the extent of harm that had been done.

"The intrigue had been carried on in such an underhanded way that even the mother had been unable to discover it." Zelie had nothing with which to reproach herself, Father Piat declares. "Overwhelmed by work and cares, she had been obliged to leave considerable initiative to the maid who was, moreover, capability personified and apparently worthy of every confidence."

Leonie was the third child. Marie and Pauline were inseparable friends. Helene, the little girl who had died when she was four, was one year younger than Leonie, and at this death Leonie was deprived of a companion. She was sickly, she was not bright. And her two older sisters were bright and charming and won all the prizes. Her mother had three other children, a father, and father-in-law and a mother-in-law living with her, and the details of her lacemaking business to consume her time.

I write as a woman, and I do not mean to disparage Mr. Martin, who was by all accounts an amazingly attractive and holy man. But I cannot help but see—and it would not be honest if I did not state it—that the position of the mother in this household was one of hard and driving toil, whereas that of the man was the more leisured one of travel, business contacts, in addition to plenty of time for the life of the spirit.

He did not lead the life of hard work that his wife and even later his daughters led. He had suffering, of course—the suffering that went with the raising of a family, the loss of little ones. But the burden of the work was on Zelie's shoulders. Later he suffered more when he lost his wife by death and his daughters to Carmel. Recognizing suffering as a vocation, he offered himself as a "victim soul." But until the end of his life he had a daughter at home. Was it because of this mystical tendency in her husband that Zelie, as she was dying, expressed the wish that her brother, too, become the legal guardian of her daughters, to safeguard their interests, their dowries, whether for marriage or the convent?

He himself realized the happiness of his existence, the pleasure of his life. It is hard for us here in America to conceive of a man retiring from business and staying at home while he is still strong and energetic, and devoting himself to his Church, his home and children. Perhaps it was on account of Leonie. But more likely he was just following the pattern of life of those times. After Zelie's death, the family had moved to Lisieux to be near Mrs. Martin's brother and his wife, so that as a couple and the parents of two daughters they could help in the raising of the Martin's children and provide more of a sense of family. With that accomplished, Mr. Martin gave up his work and, aside from some traveling, fishing, and walking trips, stayed at home. He read with his daughters, but he did not directly help in their education. Pauline and Marie seemed to take charge of that. But there was much reading together in the evening, and Gueranger's *Liturgical Year* was part of the family routine. The girls read *The Desert Fathers,* too, and perhaps the *Paradise of the Fathers,* for there was a laughing comment that they had to hide the book from their father for fear he would go and imitate these valiant men of the desert. The girls well recognized their father's holiness.

But he himself groaned in spirit and said, "My life is too easy. How am I going to achieve heaven in this way?" He evidently prayed a great deal about it and his prayer was heard. "It is a terrible thing to fall into the hands of the living God." He offered himself to suffering, and the offering of his pure heart was accepted, as we will see later.

After the death of Zelie and the removal of the family to Lisieux a few months later, Leonie was sent as a boarder to the Benedictine convent, where Celine and her two cousins, Marie and Jeanne Guerin, and later Therese herself went as day students. There is no report that she was sent home from this school, so evidently, though she was slow in her studies, she was no longer "capricious and unruly."

In a letter which Marie wrote at this time, she said, "I am hoping more from the protection of my holy mother than from my own poor efforts, to complete from on high the transformation of my poor sister . . . I notice that she has been changing daily for some time. Have you not noticed it, Father? My uncle and aunt already perceive it. I am sure it is our darling mother who is obtaining this grace for us, and I am persuaded that our Leonie will give us some consolation in the future."

She became from now on much more part of the family, and although her sick headaches made her occasionally unsociable, she no longer shut herself away from her sisters.

She was developing, too, in a most heroic way in her relations with the poor people that it had always been the habit of the family to visit and help. "She was seen," according to Father Piat, "visiting a dying woman covered with vermin, cleaning her hovel, changing her garments, comforting and cheering her, and when she was dead preparing her for burial."

When Leonie was testifying in the canonization process of the Little Flower, she said, in words that display her own humility and gratitude:

> Everything in Therese's person breathed kindness and unselfishness. She always forgot herself in order to please everybody; when she could make others happy she was in her element. Her evenness of temper was so simple and seemed so natural that it might have been thought that her continual renunciation cost her nothing. She was pleasant and courteous. Everything about her attracted people. Pride and vanity had no place in her innocent soul. She was very pretty but she seemed unaware of it. During these years when we were living together at home, I never saw

her looking into a mirror. She was delicately attentive not
to humiliate or hurt anyone. . . .

I was very touched personally by the very delicate feeling wherewith she behaved to me. I was then twenty-three
and she was only thirteen, but I was very backward in my
studies. My little sister used to teach me, using great charity
and exquisite tact so as to avoid humiliating me.

Here is a wonderful example of mother love and understanding in a letter written by Zelie Martin after she had returned from Lourdes and was dying:

Well, I am still waiting for the miracle of God's loving
kindness and omnipotence through the intercession of His
Blessed Mother. Not that I ask Him to take away my disease altogether, but only to spare me a few more years of
life, in order that I may have time to bring up my children,
and especially poor Leonie, who needs me so much and for
whom I am so sorry.

She is less favored than you others as regards to natural
endowments, but, nevertheless, she has a heart that yearns
to love and be loved, and only a mother can show her at
every moment the affection she craves, and observe her
closely enough to benefit her.

The dear child shows me unbounded tenderness; she
anticipates my wishes; nothing she does for me costs her
anything; she watches me closely to find out what will
please me; she is almost too anxious about it.

But as soon as the others ask anything of her, her face
clouds over, her expression changes in an instant. Gradually I am succeeding in making her overcome this, though
she still forgets very often.

Another letter to Pauline, away at school:

Leonie read in the Religious Weekly of a holy soul who
offered her life for the Pope and who was heard. Now
Leonie wants to die in my place and is making a novena
for that purpose. Thursday morning she said to Marie, 'I
am going to die, I don't feel well; God has heard my
prayer.' Marie laughed at her but that made Leonie, who

was entirely serious, cry. Fifteen minutes later, her tears had dried and with her volatile spirit, she had other things in mind and told us that she had to have a pair of tapestry slippers. I said to her: 'But since you want to die, that would be a waste of money!' She was silent, hoping perhaps that she would be given time to use the slippers. Perhaps she put the slippers amongst her stipulations in her prayers to die, and perhaps she promised to make them last a long time by wearing them only on big feasts.

When she was dying Zelie Martin lamented that no one would take care of her Leonie. She said to Marie, "That is not your father's role, good as he is. Who will love her like a mother?"

Marie promised her she would, and it is good to read a letter she wrote to Leonie years later when the sisters were in different convents:

"I love to know what you are doing. It may be little in appearance; but I myself am doing little things in my office of procurator, with my pears, my apples, my carrots, my beets and my radishes. But in the eyes of God there are no big things here below; there are but little things, nothings; even the most magnificent deeds are nothing in His sight. But if from our little deeds, He sees love shine, they become big indeed in His eyes."

When Pauline and Marie were in the convent, Celine and Therese tried to draw Leonie into their games, but she was the older, and often she went to her room, especially after meals, and there lacking the stimulus of companionship, she would fall asleep. The two mischievous sisters occasionally teased her and once they transformed her room into a monastic cell with texts on the walls, such as "Remember death." "Every time I hear the clock strike I am that much nearer eternity." And one flippant card, though the others must also have been put up with giggles, "When after dinner, I do not take my walk, my eyes close to the light of day."

Leonie admitted years later that she felt her inferiority.

"In meditating on Him so humiliated," she wrote to Celine, "I accept with more courage my inferiority from which I have suffered somewhat, and I know what loneliness of heart is. But at present all that rubbish scarcely touches me."

It was at the very time when Marie was preparing to enter Carmel that Leonie went to the Poor Clares in Lisieux. She had been accustomed to attending Third Order meetings with her mother, and although Marie had stated in one of her letters that Leonie was now tending to think of the religious life as her vocation, the suddenness of her move startled the family. It was a return of her old impulsiveness and secretiveness. But her health was not good enough to sustain the severe life of the Poor Clares and she returned home.

Later, in 1887, a few months before Therese entered Carmel, Leonie tried again, this time at the Convent of the Visitation at Caen. Within a few months, and before Therese herself went away, she was forced to return home once more. Her disappointment this time led her to warn her younger sister against attempting to enter so severe an order as Carmel at so young an age. Therese was not yet fifteen. A year before Mr. Martin's death in 1894 Leonie tried again. This time she remained two years, and when she left, and returned to the home of her aunt and uncle, her father was dead and all her sisters were in Carmel.

The four sisters suffered a great deal at this "failure" of Leonie. Therese wrote from Carmel to her aunt: "We were plunged into very great grief because of our poor Leonie, it was like a deathbed. The good God, wishing to try our faith, sent us no consolation and I at least could find no other prayer than that of Our Lord on the Cross: My God, my God why hast thou forsaken us: or again, as in the Agony in the Garden: My God, not my will but Thine be done. . . . I had left my letter unfinished yesterday for Marie arrived with Leonie; our emotion at sight of her was very great, we could not get her to say a word, she was weeping so: at last she was able to look at us, and all went well." Therese goes on to talk of the energy her cousin Marie has: "she is merry enough to make stones laugh" she has "virtue, self control" and "energy, the most necessary virtue; with energy one can easily arrive at the summit of perfection. If she could only give a little to Leonie, your little angel would still have enough for herself, and it would do her no harm."

It was in July, 1895, that this letter was written, and two years later, two months before her death, Therese remarks in a letter to Leonie on the good works she is engaged in, "in the world." She "wants her to be a saint." It is not until a year and three months after the death of Therese that Leonie once again enters the convent at Caen, and remains there until her death forty years later. To this day, the Visitation nuns at Caen do indeed regard Leonie, the "poor Leonie," the "darling Leonie," as a saint.

Celine was three and a half years older than Therese and was always her playmate as a child, sharing with her her deepest thoughts and desires. They had pets, silkworms, bluebirds and bantams, chickens, rabbits, and a dog. Just before Therese entered Carmel her father brought her a newborn lamb. The two girls loved flowers, and Celine had a house full of potted plants. She was lively, vivacious, steady in disposition, bright in all her lessons, more docile than Marie—the lover of freedom—and less dominant than Pauline, who always gave an impression of great strength.

Celine and Therese shared play and holidays together. They strung beads and made jewelry. They blew bubbles. They shared their books and their visits to Trouville, to Le Havre, to Paris and the famous pilgrimage to Rome. It was Celine who gave way to Therese, allowing her to enter the convent first, although she had told her father, when he offered her art lessons in Paris, that she intended one day to enter Carmel with her sisters, if the convent would accept her. She let Therese go first even though this might have endangered her own chances of entering the convent of her choice and forced her to choose another Carmel far away from home. But these girls were not entering the convent to be together. It was God alone who was the object of their search. And it was because they were drawing closer to Him that they drew closer to each other.

PART TWO

"If a little flower could speak, it seems to me that it would tell quite simply what God had done for it, without hiding any of its gifts."

VIII

Earliest Memories

How MUCH DID the Little Flower remember of her mother and of those early years of companionship with Celine? From her own writing, it is obvious that she remembered a great deal, so much that one would count it as one of the marvels of her life that she could remember so clearly little incidents which happened when she was two and three years old. There was plenty of sorrow, sickness, death, war, and conflict in the home, and there is also the impression of a life of discipline and hard work. But it was as happy a life as could be, according to the writings of Therese.

In her autobiography she divided her life before she entered Carmel into three parts, and the first part is during the life of her mother.

"I'm dividing up the course of my life before I entered Carmel into three distinct periods; the first of these is short, but rich in memories. It begins with the dawn of reason in me; it ends with the day when our dear Mother left us for a better home in heaven. God, in His goodness, allowed my mind to develop early, and impressed the memories of childhood on it so firmly that all the events I'm going to tell you about feel as if they'd happened yesterday. I suppose our Lord had a loving design in that; He wanted me to realize what a wonderful mother He'd given me, although He was so soon to reward her with a heavenly crown."

Her life, she said, was crowded with affection and her earliest memories are of smiles and caresses and of the love lavished on her by all.

While she was writing her memories, her sister Pauline gave her the letters her mother had written the elder girl while she was away in school. They contain all the little conversations between child and mother. Therese says that she remembers all the incidents referred to but she prefers to quote from her mother's letters about herself.

Baby is such a queer little creature as you never saw; she comes up and puts her arms around me and wishes I were dead. "Oh, poor little Mother," she says. "I do wish you'd die." Then, when you scold her, she explains: "Oh, but it's only because I want you to go to heaven. You told me yourself one can't go to heaven without dying." She wants to kill off her father too, when she gets really affectionate. . . .

Here's Baby coming to stroke my face with her tiny hand and give me a hug. The poor little thing stays with me all the time, and hates being parted from me. She's very fond of going into the garden, but if I'm not there she won't stay in it; she cries till she's brought back to me. . . .

Little Therese asked me the other day whether she would get into heaven. I said Yes, if she was good: and her answer was: "But if I was naughty, I suppose I'd go to hell. D'you know what I'd do then? You'd be in heaven, so I'd take refuge with you, and how would God manage to catch me then? Because you'd be holding me ever so tight in your arms." And there was a look in her eyes which told me that she really did think that: if she was in her mother's arms God wouldn't be able to do anything to her. . . .

According to St. Therese, the dawn of reason occurred when she was two and a half years old! According to Pascal, in his discourse on the passions of love, "The life of man is miserably short. It is reckoned from his first entry into the world. I should be inclined to count it only from the birth of reason and from the time that reason begins to stir within us, which does not generally take place till the age of twenty."

Most theologians now place the dawn of reason at about seven or eight, differing of course from child to child. First Communion is generally permitted when a child has reached the age of reason; that is, when he is able to tell the difference between bread that he eats to feed his body and the "supersubstantial" bread of Holy Communion. This is a reasonable act of faith, something that it is reasonable to believe from the account in the Gospels of the words of Christ at the Last Supper reported in St. John 17, and by St. Paul in his second letter to the Corinthians, chapter 11.

There was an early incident in the life of Therese which illustrates this ability of children to see into the depths of things. "Do you love God enough to want to suffer for your brother who does not love him? Will you do without this refreshing drink after a hot walk, just to show you will suffer a little for him, sharing in Christ's sufferings?" This was a question put to her by Marie one time, and when the child assented, Marie saw to it that her thirst was quenched anyway.

That word of Christ on the Cross, "I thirst," was always in her mind when she was older. She said she wanted to give him souls, to assuage that thirst for man's love.

Whenever she did something wrong, she was very conscious of it and would run and confess it; for instance, that she had pushed and smacked her sister, that she had torn some of the wall paper. She can remember being pert to her father and pettish to her mother. Once her father had asked her for a kiss. "Come and get it," she told him. He, of course, showed his displeasure. Another time when her mother came to take her out of the crib, she hid under the covers. "I don't want anyone to look at me," she complained. How often we have seen our children act the same way. But how quickly Therese tried to make up for it. When her parents showed their displeasure, "the whole house echoed with my cries of contrition."

She wrote of her early love for her sisters, for Marie who let her stay in the room when she taught Celine and was always giving her little presents; how constantly she thought of

Pauline who was still away at school, and how when she heard Pauline was going to be a nun she made up her mind that she, too, would be a nun. "That is one of the first things I can remember, and I have never changed my mind since."

Then "darling Leonie" who took care of her when the others went for walks and who sang her to sleep at night. Celine was the favorite though, and Therese had so many memories of her that she did not know how to choose which to tell about. They understood each other perfectly, she said, but Therese declared that she herself was more lively and much less naive than her older sister. Celine was always good, but Zelie called Therese a little madcap, bright but not docile as her sister, obstinate and proud, and even vain, wishing to wear a sleeveless dress which would "make her look prettier." But Therese said her faults were corrected very early, and once corrected did not return. She had only good example around her and she said she needed to be told only once not to do a thing for her "not to want to do it again."

Her mother wrote in one letter, "Even Therese wants to start making sacrifices now. Marie has given each of the little ones a chaplet on which they can keep count of their good deeds. They have real spiritual conferences together. It is most amusing. Celine asked the other day: 'How can God get into such a little Host?' Therese answered her: 'It's not surprising since our Lord is Almighty.' 'What does Almighty mean?' 'It means He can do anything he wants.' But the most charming thing of all is to see Therese slip her hand into her pocket time and time again, and move a bead along as she makes some sacrifice."

The two children were together all the time, they shared their toys and their pets. After dinner in the evening they used to play with two bantam chickens in the corner of the fireplace. One morning when her elders went to dress Therese, they found she had gotten into bed with Celine. Hugging her close, Therese said, "We are like the little white chickens, we must always be together." Therese poured out her affection on her sister as she did on her mother, and if Celine left the table first, Therese would go without her dessert to follow her, so that they could play together.

Celine used to bring blessed bread home from Mass to her little sister who was still too young for the long service on Sunday. Once when she had not brought any, Therese demanded that she make some at once. Celine went to the loaf in the cupboard and cutting off a little square, made the sign of the cross over it and said a prayer. The child was satisfied.

Therese remembers a dream she had at the age of three and which, she said, left a very deep impression. She was walking alone in the garden and suddenly she saw "two horrible little devils near the arbor, dancing on a barrel of lime with amazing agility in spite of having heavy irons on their feet." They looked at her with flaming eyes and then, as if overcome by fear, threw themselves in the twinkling of an eye to the bottom of the barrel. They escaped in some mysterious way, and ran off to hide in the linen room which opened on to the garden. "When I saw how cowardly they were I put my fears aside and went over to the window to see what they were up to. There the little wretches were, running around and around the table, and not knowing how to escape my gaze. From time to time they came nearer, still very agitated, to peep through the window; then when they saw that I was still there, they began racing about again in abject misery."

She does not give much importance to this dream but she said she felt that God made use of it to show her that anyone in a state of grace had no need to fear.

"I was so happy at this age," she wrote, "not only because I was beginning to enjoy life but also because virtue had begun to appeal to me. I think my dispositions were the same then as they are now."

She was beginning, even at that very early age, to see what the spiritual life meant, the series and successions of definite choices, the preference which means the life of love, the ordering of every little thing in life as though we were "practicing the presence of God." "What would He have me to do?" "Speak Lord, for Thy servant heareth." Samuel, St.

Paul, all the saints had that attitude, that attraction to the good, that sense of the importance of the present moment.

She was already self-controlled, she wrote. She did not complain if any of her things were taken from her, and if ever she were unjustly accused she kept silence rather than excuse herself. And yet she adds, "There was no real virtue in this on my part for it came naturally." The struggle had not really begun. Virtue was pleasant.

Those were sunny years of childhood with delightful memories. Her father used to take the children to the pavilion where he kept his fishing tackle and books; he took them for walks on Sunday and then her mother was with them. She remembers the wheat fields studded with poppies and cornflowers and daisies. "She loved," she said—she who was to wall herself in at the age of fifteen in a severely cloistered order—"she loved far distances, wide spaces and trees." Her whole soul was steeped in beauty and love, and her own happy nature made life all the more delightful. For four and a half years, the whole world was sunny for her.

And then came her mother's illness and those last weeks of Zelie's life on earth. A friend used to come to the house every day to take Celine and Therese away from this house overshadowed with tragedy. How distraught the family was, how they hastened to get rid of the two little children, to take them away from the sound and sight of pain, is shown by one small incident which Therese recounts. The two little girls told the friend one morning that they had not yet said their morning prayers, and when the friend arrived at her own home, she put them in a large room and went away leaving them to pray. "Mother is not like that," Therese said. "She always says our prayers with us." All they thought of during the day was their mother, and when they were given apricots they saved them for her, though their poor mother was too ill by then to eat anything.

Therese tells how the ceremony of Extreme Unction impressed her, how she heard her father weeping, and then the sight of her mother's dead body. Her father lifted the child in his arms and said, "My little one, here kiss your darling mother for the last time." She remembered her mother's cold forehead, she remembered hearing conversation and seeing a lot that they wanted to keep from her. Once she found herself all alone in the hall, looking at the long coffin which was left standing on its end in the corridor. It was big and gloomy to the tiny girl.

And now Therese's natural gaiety left her, and the second part of her life—the saddest she calls it—was to begin. This lasted from the time she was four and a half until she was fourteen. She was no longer lively and open, but diffident and oversensitive, crying if anyone looked at her. She could not bear to be anywhere but in the intimacy of her own family, where she could be herself. Her father and her two oldest sisters overwhelmed her with loving kindness; both Pauline and Marie were the kindest and most unselfish of mothers to her.

She would not have lived, she wrote, if she had not had this warmth and kindness.

Following the last wish of Zelie that her sister-in-law Celine Guerin should watch over her family of five girls when she was gone, the family moved to Lisieux from Alençon where the entire married life of the Martins had been lived. Like all children, Therese loved change, she said, and so she enjoyed the move. She remembered arriving at her uncle's house in the evening and finding her little cousins, Jeanne and Marie, and her Aunt Celine and Uncle Isidore all standing at the door waiting for them. They, too, were filled with love and warmth, and now there were seven girls growing up together.

The new home which the Martins had rented not too far away was called Les Buissonnets, which means "the shrubbery," from the trim gardens at the front and back of the house. It was in a quiet part of the town.

"I was quite charmed by the house," she writes, "and my imagination was carried away by the distant view from the belvedere." It was from the windows of this "penthouse," as it were, that she and her sister Celine used to look out at night and feel an overwhelming joy in contemplating the stars and skies and talking of the supernatural life.

In spite of her description of herself as withdrawn and oversensitive, she goes on to write, "This lovely house was to be the setting for so many delightful times for all of us. Everywhere else I felt lost, and used to cry and miss Mother, but there my little heart opened out and I could greet life with a smile."

Pauline, whom she called her little mother, was always there to kiss her awake. Therese said her prayers kneeling beside her big sister and there, too, she learned to read. The first word she read was "heaven." Doubtless there was much talk of heaven, to remind the little one that though man is but dust and unto dust he must return, still he is also a creature of body and soul, and the soul immediately flies to God at death, and looks forward to being united to the dear body at the resurrection of the dead. This, the substance of the faith taught to Catholic children, must have been specially poignant in view of her early acquaintance with sickness, suffering, death, and corruption.

The very fact that children come face to face with death and suffering early, makes for that paradox, "rejoicing in tribulation," that the New Testament speaks of. Therese suffered, hovered on the verge of tears, could not bear to go abroad, was hypersensitive. The light of life seemed to have gone out with her mother, and yet she spoke of delightful times in their new home, of visiting their cousins and going on holidays.

"I die, yet behold I live," St. Paul says. One has to experience this to write about it. In cold words, it is hard to convey this sense of tears and joy, soft rain and sunshine.

The house at Les Buissonnets was a charming one although there was no electricity, gas, or water. There was an open hearth in the kitchen with kettles hanging over it and a spit on which roasts and fowl could be cooked. The stove was heated with charcoal. Breakfast chocolate was only for the young.

When they got older, the girls had onion soup for breakfast! On that ground floor which opened out into the garden, there was a large kitchen and dining room and a sitting room, but it was the kitchen which was most used. There they played games and read aloud together in the evening, and Therese enjoyed baking potatoes on the hot stones. It was there that Celine painted her miniatures and oil paintings, and Marie made lace for a priest's alb—a task which took her two years. This alb was worn later by Cardinal Pacelli before he became Pope Pius XII. After Pauline left for the convent in 1882, Marie became the mistress of this new home for nine years, and after she, in turn, went to the Carmel, it was Celine who managed affairs.

New Year's Day was the time for formal visiting among these French families, and the girls pitied their relatives, the Guerins, who had to make sixty calls to their four, in order to greet relatives and friends.

Every afternoon Mr. Martin took his youngest daughter for a walk, to pay a visit to the Blessed Sacrament in each of the churches in the town. When she was five she visited Carmel for the first time and heard her father tell how the holy nuns spent their time in prayer behind the grille, and never went out for walks, never set foot outside their walls.

After the walk she used to finish her lessons, and then she could play in the garden, the large rear garden where the family spent much of their time in good weather. She did there what so many of us have done as children. She mixed up bits of bark and flowers and made strange-smelling, and stranger-looking concoctions which she brought to her father in one of her prettiest doll dishes to taste, and he would pretend to sip the strange brew.

She loved, she said, to grow flowers, and in a little niche in the garden wall, she set up altars which she decorated. She went fishing with her father and had a little rod of her own, but she got tired of waiting for a bite and used to go aside in the flowery grass to sit and listen, and think deep thoughts, indeed, for a child. There was the murmur of the wind in the grasses and trees and sometimes the sound of music from the town, martial music which made her feel sad, she wrote. She felt she was in a place of exile even though she was sitting by her dearly loved father, and she loved to dream of heaven.

A very real melancholy used to seize her when she surveyed the sandwiches, which looked so good when Pauline was making them and later looked so wilted and discolored with the jam spreading through the bread.

Some time later, when she made her first Communion, she prayed that the Lord would turn all sweet things bitter for her, so that she would not be counting on things of this earth but would be turning to heaven. It seemed that already there was growth in her soul. God was already stripping her of a little child's greediness, the greediness that we seldom get over in this life, feeling as we do that eating is one of the licit pleasures.

Eating and drinking with others is a communion, and the fact that our Lord left Himself to us in bread and wine makes eating a divine as well as a human act, so when the Little Flower talks about her distaste for the picnic lunch, one may well see that there was a natural melancholy of temperament there, a sadness of the body as well as of the soul.

She was delighted at this time, too, with the evidence of the power of God when she was caught in a thunderstorm with her father, and saw a thunderbolt fall in a nearby meadow. She was not frightened at all, though her father was and hastened her through a field of daisies which were taller than she and all glistening with rain. He had to carry both her and his fishing tackle that day.

At this early age she became conscious of the misery of the poor, and compassion flowed through her when she met them on her walks with her father.

From the very beginning she was brought into contact with them. She tells in the first chapter of her book about Leonie's first Holy Communion. It was the custom in those days to dress another child and feast her together with the daughter of the family, and at the grand dinner in the evening the young guest had the place of honor. In the first chapter, too, she speaks of how she was the one delegated to give alms when they met, as they often did, people who were poor and ragged. In the second chapter she tells of one old crippled man who filled her with a sense of pity at his helplessness and pain and how she offered him some money which he refused with a wry smile.

I can't describe my emotions; here was this man I should have liked to comfort and console, and instead of that I'd injured his feelings. I dare say the poor cripple guessed what was passing through my mind, because he turned back to smile at me. How would it be to give him the cake Papa had just bought for me? No, I hadn't the courage; but I did wish I could offer him something, something it would have been impossible to refuse; I felt so terribly sorry for him. Then I remembered having been told that on your first Communion day you could get any prayer granted. That was a comforting thought; I was only six years old then, but when I made my first Communion I would remember the poor man. That promise I kept, five years later, and I hope the prayer was answered; a prayer God himself had inspired; a prayer for one of His suffering members.

I came to love God more and more as I grew up and often offered my heart to Him in the words Mother had taught me. I used to try hard to please Jesus in everything I did and never offend Him.

Immediately after writing these things, she tells of a fault of temper she committed against a maid who laughed at her. Therese was considered too young to go to the evening May devotions at the time. So she decorated a little altar in the house with flowers and the stumps of two candles which the maid had given her. Delighted as all children are to be playing with fire, she was the one to light the candles while the maid did the praying, saying a *Memorare,* St. Bernard's famous prayer to our Lady which is supposed to obtain for us any favor we ask. Every time the maid started her prayers she burst out laughing, and since Therese was allowed to burn only two matches and she saw them burning out before she was able to light her candles, she lost her temper and stamped her foot, shouting, "You wicked Victoire!"

It must have been seldom that such a thing happened because the maid stopped laughing immediately, looking at the child in great surprise. Then Victoire showed the treat she had saved for her, two new candles! When she brought them out from under her apron, Therese felt ashamed and remorseful and cried indeed. She was so ashamed of herself that she resolved she said, never to let such a thing happen again.

There is never too small an incident for Therese to mention in her memories, knowing that we can all of us match them, but not, perhaps, draw the same lesson.

IX

Confession and Communion

IT HAS BEEN CUSTOMARY since the reign of Pope Pius X, now a canonized saint, for children to make their first Confession and Communion at about the age of seven or eight, when they reach the second grade in school. At the time of the first Confessions, which are heard the day before the great day of Communion, some of the children are afraid and some pretend to be if they are not. At any rate, it almost seems that as much emphasis is placed on one sacrament as on the other. In St. Therese's time, however, children could go to Confession whenever their elders decided they knew what they were talking about, knew right from wrong, and had "reached the age of reason." In the case of the Little Flower, she was permitted to go at the age of five. Six years before she received the Body and Blood of the Lord!

> My first confession—that is one of my most delightful memories. You'd prepared me for it so well, dear Mother, explaining to me that I was really going to tell God about my sins, not just a man. That sank in, and I made my confession full of the spirit of faith; I even asked you, "If it's God I'm going to talk to in his person, ought I to tell M. Ducellier that I love him with my whole heart?"

What could this child of five have had to confess?

She could confess to anger at the maid for teasing her, to slapping her sister Celine, to acting pettishly with her father and mother, and so on. It was clear enough to her in those early days. Later she suffered from scruples and a constant sense of guilt. Father Hans von Balthasar in his *Therese of Lisieux,* writes that her family had done extremely well in not blunting her fine and delicate sense of sin. They helped her always to do the hard thing, the more perfect thing, not to justify herself when she was accused, not to complain when things were taken from her. She saw her own constant failures. She confesses to feeling injured on one occasion when she had watered her sister's plants and then had not received thanks. She confesses that she wanted to be admired, wanted to wear a sleeveless dress so that she would be the more admired. This happened while her mother was still alive, before she was four, when her sister was dressing her to go visiting. The mother called out from her window where she was making lace, "Do not put the sleeveless dress on her," and Therese thought, "but I would look much nicer in that one."

Therese said she went to Confession on the eve of all the great feasts. She knew, after all, something of the world. Later, too, after her illness her father took her on a round of visits. One is reminded of Jane Austen's books and the visiting back and forth at country homes, in such stories as *Mansfield Park* and *Emma.*

God, in his mercy, has given me little knowledge of the world; only just enough to make me despise it and want to keep away from it; and I suppose I really saw it for the first time during this stay at Alençon. So much opportunity to enjoy myself and be happy there; everybody entertained me, petted me, admired me; in fact, for a whole fortnight I trod the primrose path. And all this, I confess, had its attractions for me; how rightly does the Book of Wisdom warn us that the sorcery of the world's vanities can bewitch even unworldly minds! At ten years old, one's mind is easily dazzled, and I look upon it as a great grace that we didn't stay longer at Alençon. Our friends there were worldly people, who had the knack of serving God and at the same time enjoying, to the full, the good things of earth.

The thought of death seldom crossed their minds; and yet death has come to so many of them, those people who were so young, so rich, so happy when I knew them! It intrigues me to go back, in memory, to the enchanted world they lived in, and to wonder where they are now—what satisfaction do they derive now from the châteaux and the parks where I used to see them enjoying all that life had to give them? It makes you realize that there's nothing but frustration and labour lost, here under the sun; that nothing is worthwhile except loving God with your whole heart and being poor in spirit as long as this life lasts.

Perhaps our Lord wanted to prepare me for his first visit to my soul in the Blessed Sacrament, by showing me what the world was really like; in pledging myself to follow him, I was to make a real choice between two paths.

She tells, too, of people remarking on her beauty when she visited at the seashore every year with her aunt and cousins, and other remarks about her appearance made when she was at church with her father. Later, when because of her illness she was being tutored in the home of a friend, women of the world came to visit. She was thirteen, and her father wanted her not only to have instruction but also to be brought into contact with the outside world.

"Visitors were often shown into the quaintly furnished room where I sat surrounded with my books, and though conversation was carried on, as far as possible, by my governess's mother, I did not succeed in learning much while the visits lasted. Though seemingly absorbed in my work, little escaped my attention, even of what it would have been far better I should not hear."

When one considers the conversations one has overheard as a child, the scandals, the repeating of others' faults, the knowledge of sex which a child gains by listening to adult conversation, one can well imagine that this bright little child learned a great deal that was not in the books doled out to her.

Therese confesses how sweet was the flattery she heard, and how easy it was "to go astray along the world's seductive

paths. Without doubt the sweetness which it offers one somewhat advanced in virtues is always mingled with bitterness,
nor can the immense void of such a soul's desires be filled by
the flattery of a moment." In other words, why tempt me with
so little? Therese's desires were boundless, she wanted everything in the way of love. She tells the story on herself of how
when Leonie brought her own dolls and toys to her two
younger sisters, thinking herself too old for them, and the
girls started to choose, Celine modestly took one article from
the lot, but her youngest sister seized all that remained saying, "I choose all."

She chose the All, and nothing less would satisfy her.
Yet there were tentative reachings towards human love.
Therese was taught at home until she was eight, and then she
went to school to the Benedictines in Lisieux for the next four
years, as a day student. Celine had been going there for two
years, so it was not too great a plunge for Therese from her
sheltered home into the schoolroom. Still, it was hard. At the
school, seeing the other girls especially devoted to one or the
other of the mistresses, she tried to imitate them but "never
succeeded in winning special favor." Another time she chose
two little girls as friends, and when one, evidently the more
favored of the two, stayed home while sick, Therese thought
of her a great deal. She showed her great happiness at the
girl's return to school but only met with rebuffs. Her advances
were met with indifference. "I felt this very keenly, and I no
longer sought an affection which had proved so inconstant."

In one of the passages from her story omitted by its first
editor, Mother Agnes, Therese says her years at the Benedictine convent school were the "saddest of my life; if I had
not had with me my dear Celine, I would not have been able
to stay there a single month without falling sick."

She confesses that she was ready to give her heart to both
teacher and pupils, that she was looking for an object of affection. She was hungry for love, in spite of the love she enjoyed
at home with her cousins. The heart is never satisfied. Given
a chance, she would have indulged in what is so vulgarly

termed a "crush" on a school mistress or schoolmate. And we know to what depths of evil such emotions, fostered innocently enough, may lead.

Therese learned much at an early age and this child knew what evil was. She knew too how weak she was, and how it was our Lord Himself who was always protecting her, withdrawing the stone from her path so that she should not stumble.

What if later she did have that assurance of a good priest who heard confessions at Carmel, that as far as he could discern from hearing her confessions, she had never committed a grievous sin? His statement did not mean that she was without the venial sins, the imperfections, the ability to sin, the capacity for sin—and an immense capacity at that, as immense as her capacity for love. She had plumbed the heights and the depths, this child!

But Father von Balthasar complains that, due to this indiscreet remark of her confessor's, Therese lost that sense of sin which is so necessary if the Christian is to feel pity and responsibility. "Certain of the central mysteries remain unacknowledged in her theology," he writes. "The mystery of bearing sins, and of solidarity in sin, the mystery of how love may be coupled with an awareness of sin, above all the mystery of confession."

Yet her realization of the capacity of each one of us for sin must have been enormous. And who is there who has felt the breath of sin about him, who has felt the stirring in his depths, the monster, the tempter, who has realized the depths into which he might have fallen, indeed might still fall, and has not felt such contamination by this realization of sin that he needed the reassurance of the priest hearing his confession that he had not sinned but merely been tempted to sin?

For such an individual there might never have been an immediate occasion of sin. There might never have been a specific temptation, an opportunity, one might say, of sinning. But what youth has ever been lonely, and apart, and far from the world of glitter and glamor and excitement and joy without wishing that the opportunities of choice between sin and virtue, between good and evil, might come to him. This may be a temptation of youth, deprived of the opportunity of great choices. But it may also be the great hunger of a woman who feels her capacity for human love.

The Little Flower herself spoke of the goodness of the Father who had removed all obstacles from the path of His child, knowing her capacity for sin, her danger of falling. She well knew her weakness, she well knew the world. She recognized and said over and over again that it was because of her parents, her sisters, her home life, the training she had received, and finally her life in the convent that she had been saved from falling into the most appalling depths of sin.

Of what sin was she, Therese, not capable! "Suppose that [a] father, knowing that a large stone lies on his son's path, anticipates the danger and, unseen by anyone, hastens to remove it. Unconscious of the accident from which such tender forethought has saved him, the son will not show any mark of gratitude for it, or feel the same love for his father as he would have done had he been cured of some grievous wound by his father. But if he came to learn the whole truth, would he not love his father all the more?"

But she also suffered intensely from scruples and for so long that it was a neurosis, like the need to be forever washing one's hands. She was tempted to vanity and wept, and then wept because she had wept. Vanity may seem to be only a slight sin, but to what depths vanity has led many a woman, perhaps only a woman can know. The vanity of Eve, that desire to exercise power, to seduce, to drag down!

Just as this child longed for the martyrdom of a Joan of Arc, an Ignatius of Antioch, as an atonement, as a way of showing her love, so also she recognized the capacity to sin which she possessed. Her love, she felt, should be greater than that of a Magdalene, because she had been prevented from sin by a loving Father who knew her weakness, knew to what depths she could have fallen. She gave up, too, her desires for great and noble deeds.

In other words, she expected nothing of herself, she was "the little grain of sand," trampled underfoot, forgotten, and God would do it all in making her a saint, because He wanted it. He wanted just such a saint as she was to become, because she was ordinary, just like many another girl, a child of comfortably situated, hard-working people. She was one of "the people." When she spoke of herself as a "little flower," a comparison her father had made, it was of a common, ordinary and fragile little flower of the spring, common as grass, that she was thinking.

Therese had no scruples until she had made her first Holy Communion, so she was able to rejoice with a clear heart at that time. She had recovered from a dangerous illness, mental or nervous, which affected her whole body with fever and weakness; she had been taken on holidays to country homes and to the seashore, where she enjoyed bathing and shrimping and donkey rides and other childish sports. Then came the time to prepare for her first Communion. "It seems to me I could not have been better prepared," she writes and so conveys a sense of the leisure for thought and prayer and the savoring of life's great occasions which seems so lacking to us today. Pauline in her convent had prepared a little booklet called *Three Months of Preparation for First Communion,* and Therese found there "an attractive method which prepared me gradually and thoroughly." It sounds from her description of it a most flowery affair, counting sacrifices and acts of love as so many flowers to line a nest to make a cradle to hold the Holy Child.

Every evening she spent a long time with her other sister, Marie, who "was so eloquent that her noble and generous spirit seemed to pass into mine. As the warriors of old trained their children in the profession of arms, so she trained me for the battle of life, and roused my ardour by pointing out the victors' glorious palm." Then came a period of retreat at the Benedictine Convent where the number of children was small enough so the mistresses could give special attention to each child. It was a retreat with instructions, and Therese took

copious notes, she said. She followed the Divine Office just as
the nuns did, and this meant long hours in chapel where the
nuns sang the psalms and antiphons of the different hours of
the day. Matins, Lauds, Prime, Terce, Sext, None, Vespers
and Compline, a collection which in a week covers the entire
Psalter, with the addition of scriptural readings and lessons
from the early fathers, St. Basil, St. John Chrysostom, St.
Augustine, St. Jerome, St. Ambrose, and so on, not to speak
of hymns and canticles that enlarge the heart with their
beauty. She must already have had some knowledge of Latin, this
child of eleven. After all, she entered Carmel at fifteen and
there the nuns recited the Office, just as the Benedictines did.

At last the day came, that greatest of all days for me;
even the tiniest details of that visit to heaven have left their
imprint on my memory, not to be described. To what glad-
ness I awoke; how gently and how reverently they embraced me, the mistresses and the older girls who were
there! The big room, and the dresses laid out there, white
as snowflakes, which we put on, one after another. . . .
And above all the chapel, and that lovely hymn, chanted
in the fresh morning air, "O altar of God, where the angels
are hovering." But I don't want to go into details; there are
scents which you can't expose to the air without their losing their fragrance, and there are experiences of the soul
which you can't express in human language without losing
their inner meaning, their heavenly meaning. They are like
that white stone given to the faithful warrior, on which a
name is written, known only to him who receives it. What
comfort it brought to me, that first kiss our Lord imprinted
on my soul! A lover's kiss; I knew that I was loved, and I,
in my turn, told him that I loved him, and was giving myself to him for all eternity. It was a long time now since he
had made any demands on me; there had been no struggles,
no sacrifices; we exchanged looks, he and I, insignificant
though I was, and we had understood one another. And
now it wasn't a question of looks; something had melted
away, and there were no longer two of us—Therese had

simply disappeared, like a drop lost in the ocean; Jesus only was left, my Master, my King. Hadn't I begged him to take away my liberty, because I was so afraid of the use I might make of it; hadn't I longed, weak and helpless as I was, to be united once for all with that divine Strength?

So deep was my joy, so overpowering, that I couldn't contain myself; before long, tears of happiness were pouring down my cheeks . . .

Some have called attention to the sexual element in such language. It is the language of love, of course, and the only way to describe the love of God is in terms of the most intense human love, that between man and woman. One does not have to experience it to know what it means. Nicholas Berdyaev states that the keenest and most intense love between man and women is not dependent on sexual intercourse. This love which makes all seem new is already described in the Old Testament as a wedding, and there has never been a greater song of love written than the Canticle of Canticles.

Did Therese really mean what she wrote?

"Always I have said to the good God: O God, I will listen to You gladly; I beg of You to answer me when I humbly ask You: what is the truth. Make me see things as they are. Nothing should blind us to that." "Is this pure love truly in my heart? Is my infinite longing not a dream, and an illusion? Oh, if it is, then enlighten me! You know that I am seeking the truth." "All imaginings mean nothing to me. I can only nourish myself on the truth." "It seems to me that humility is truth. I do not know whether I am humble. But I do know that I seek the truth in everything." On the very day of her death she said, "Yes, I believe that I have always sought after truth."

In the light of these statements one can believe that this language of love which St. Therese used was spoken in truth and that she enjoyed raptures of love.

She made her second Communion on Ascension Day and repeated again and again to herself, "I live, now not I, but

Christ liveth in me." With these words of St. Paul, she said,
a most ardent desire for Holy Communion grew in her. The
great feasts when she would be allowed to receive Communion seemed very far apart. On the eve of one of them,
when Marie, who was helping her prepare, spoke of suffering, she told her little sister that in all probability God would
not require her to walk by that road. The next day after Communion, Therese said, these words came back to her, bringing
with them a conviction that she would have many a cross to
bear. "Then a wave of consolation swept over my soul—of
such consolation as in all my life I have never known. Suffering became my treasure."

Not long after that Therese received the sacrament of Confirmation, and made another retreat to prepare for it. "Speaking to Celine, her fourteen-year-old sister, during this retreat,
of the manner in which the Holy Ghost takes possession of a
soul in this Sacrament of Love, her words were so inflamed,
and her look became suddenly so ardent, that her sister, unable to endure it, lowered her eyes and withdrew, filled with
a sense of the supernatural she never forgot." (*The Spirit of
St. Therese,* by the Carmelites of Lisieux.)

It was after these experiences that she speaks of trying
without success to form attachments for one or other of her
teachers or schoolmates. The heart filled with love searches
for someone on whom to bestow it.

> Lucky for me that I had so little gift for making myself
> agreeable; it has preserved me from dangers. I shall always
> be grateful to our Lord for turning earthly friendships into
> bitterness for me, because, with a nature like mine, I could
> so easily have fallen into a snare and had my wings clipped;
> and then how should I have been able to "Fly away and
> find rest." I don't see how it's possible for a heart given
> over to such earthly affections to attain any intimate union
> with God. I can't speak from experience, because this im-
> moderate love of creatures is a poison-draught which has
> always been kept away from my lips, but I'm sure I'm right
> about this—I've seen so many souls go that way. They're

like the poor moths; dazzled by the lure of this rushlight, they fly into it and burn their wings, only to come back later into the soft radiance of that true love which is divine. They need fresh wings, brighter and more nimble than ever, if they're to fly back to our Lord, the divine Fire that burns without consuming what it burns. He knew, evidently, that I was too weak to be exposed to such temptations; if once I'd allowed this false light to dazzle me, it might have burned me outright.

If that didn't happen, if I only found bitterness where other souls find attraction, and have to resist the attraction by fidelity to grace, that was no credit to me. It was only God's mercy that preserved me from giving myself up to the love of creatures; without that, I might have fallen as low as St. Mary Magdalen did. I find such comfort in those penetrating words of our Lord to Simon the Pharisee: "He loves little, who has little forgiven him." But I, you say, owed him little? On the contrary, I owe him more than the Magdalen herself; he remitted my sins beforehand, as it were, by not letting me fall into them. Oh dear, I wish I could explain exactly what I feel about it.

As I understand her, St. Therese is teaching the necessity of loving God first, and then "all these things shall be added unto you." All these happy loves of earth, family, friends, husband, children. "Seek ye first the kingdom of God, *and all these things shall be added unto you.*" This is blind faith, a naked faith in love. A little child is told these things early, and with his trusting heart and open mind he accepts these truths though he has not experienced them.

Therese takes no credit to herself. It is all God's doing. "Behold the handmaid of the Lord, be it done unto me according to Thy word." Knowing that it is all God's work in her soul, she can say with the Psalmist—"Enlarge my heart that thou mayest enter in." "Make me *desire* to walk in the way of Thy commandments." The emphasis is on God, and His grace. She, of course, responds to this grace, and grace, which is defined as "participation in the divine life," grows in her, so she can say, "now not I, but Christ in me." It made her infinitely daring in her desire to be a saint. "God would not give us these desires if he did not wish to satisfy them" she writes.

Here is one of those paragraphs in which Mother Agnes, in rewriting it, inserts sentences of her own, such as "There, where strong souls find joy, and are faithful in practicing detachment, I found only bitterness."

Either Mother Agnes missed the point or she was afraid readers would be repelled or frightened by the austerity of such teaching. What—have no human affection whatever? Not love friends and relatives? The bleakness of such an outlook is indeed frightening. But it is part of the tremendous affirmation of faith in love on the part of Therese. She was ready to stake her life in this renunciation of love. We must be ready to give up everything. We must have already given it up, before God can give it back transfigured, supernaturalized. "He who does not hate father, mother, sister, brother, for my name's sake, is not worthy to be my disciple."

He is indeed a jealous lover. He wants all.

Beneath the stilted, flowery writing of the time, this creature of truth well knew what she was saying. She has a strong, clear sight of the temptations which surround the heart desirous of loving and of being loved, but before she could be in danger, she said, temptation was removed from her. Before she could even find "delectation in temptation," as St. Francis de Sales quaintly puts it, it turned to bitterness in her mouth. But she did have the long attack of scruples which was enough to make her unlovable to those around her.

X

Reading

WHAT WERE THE BOOKS that made up the background for the life of this home at Lisieux? "There is much I could tell you about our winter evenings at home. After a game of draughts, you [Pauline] or Marie used to read aloud from the *Liturgical Year,* and then a few pages from some other instructive and interesting book. During this time I always sat on papa's knee. When the reading was over, he would rock me gently, my head pillowed on his breast, and would sing in his beautiful voice some soothing melody as if to lull me to sleep."

It is a happiness to read of this strong unashamed family love, so difficult for the Anglo-Saxon to express. Between Jansenism and the smattering of psychology that people as a whole have gone in for, grave and ugly accusations have been made in relation to family love, love between brother and sister, between father and daughter, mother and child. The perversion of the best is rottenness indeed, and people of this day have looked down into the depths, the black depths of perverse love, and realizing its horror have fled from love expressed in tenderness. And yet the desire for love is so strong, the desire for tenderness is so inherent that there is a frank and unashamed seeking after sex as an opportunity to enjoy this all too human need of tenderness.

And what good teaching Therese got from Pauline! "One day I expressed surprise that God does not give an equal amount of glory to all the inhabitants of heaven—I was afraid they would not all be quite happy. You sent me to fetch Papa's big tumbler, and putting it beside my tiny thimble, filled both with water and asked me which seemed the fuller. I replied that one was as full as the other; it was impossible to pour more water into either of them as they could not hold it. In this way you made it clear to me that in Heaven the least of the Blessed does not envy the happiness of the greatest; and by bringing the highest mysteries down to the level of my understanding, you gave my soul the food it required."

Another time Pauline and Therese were sitting on a lonely rock by the seashore. It was Therese's first holiday by the sea and she was awed and impressed by its majesty. The sun was setting and left a glow of light on the water, and Pauline remarked to the little girl that it was like God's grace illumining the way. The father talked to her, too, of serious things, just as though she were a grownup girl, as she puts it, and she would say to him, "It is certain, Papa, that if you spoke like that to the great men who govern the country, they would make you its king, and France would be happier than she ever has been. But you yourself would be unhappy, for such is the lot of kings, and besides you would no longer be my King alone, so I am glad they do not know you!"

They read history and the story of Joan of Arc, and her heart swelled with love of her country, to which, however, she did not wish to sacrifice her father.

They read the *Lives of the Fathers of the Desert,* and they pretended they were hermits, she and her cousin Marie, who was her age; while one prayed, the other would be engaged in active work in the garden, raising a patch of corn and a few vegetables. As they walked through the town they continued their game; wishing to close their eyes to the things of the world around them, they fell over some boxes of a grocer and scattered his goods on the pavement. When they were scolded by the grocer and their maid Jeanne, the two girls forgot their dignity and ran off at full speed. One can see them, these little girls, with their hair down their backs, laughing and embarrassed at the same time. It is told of

Therese somewhere that she was a good mimic and delighted her friends with her imitations. One can hear her interpreting the tradesman, the hermits, and the maid.

She was gay and carefree at home and with her cousins, but she was timid abroad, and when she began school at the Abbey, the Benedictine convent in Lisieux, she did not find it easy. Leonie had gone there before her, but now had left school; Celine was some classes ahead of her.

All the girls in her class were older than she and one of them, a fourteen-year-old found many ways to make her suffer. Therese was first in her class, and the other girl "paid me out in a thousand ways." Therese says she was not advanced enough in virtue to rise above this persecution and spent much time in tears. But she was advanced enough not to tell about her troubles to her sisters and could only write about them years later.

Every day she brought home good marks and was petted by her father, and once a week she received a silver piece for her poor-box. "Such kindnesses were in my case a real necessity: the Little Flower needed to strike its tender roots deeper and deeper into the dearly loved garden of home, for nowhere else could it find the nourishment it required."

Among all children, there are those lonely ones "who do not know how to play like the other children, [and] I felt myself a dull companion, and though I tried my best to do as they did, it was always without success." However she could tell stories, "making them up out of her head as she went along," and often during the recreation she won the friendship of the other children by this ability to tell about the books she had been reading.

Therese, however, felt lonely at school in the midst of crowds of other children and happy at home with her sisters and her cousins. She did, however, read a great deal. "They chose for me books that were suitable to my age, interesting, yet providing food for both mind and heart. The time set apart for this, my favorite recreation, was carefully limited, so that it became an occasion of much self-sacrifice, as no sooner had the time elapsed, than I made a point of instantly putting the book down, even in the middle of the most absorbing passage." What self-discipline in a child of eight!

"With regard to the impressions produced on me by these books, I must frankly own that, in reading certain tales of chivalry, I did not always understand the realities of life; and in my admiration for the patriotic deeds of the heroines of France, especially of the Venerable Joan of Arc [she had not as yet been canonized, and one wonders what Therese made of the actions of the Bishops who condemned Joan], I longed to do what they had done. Then I received what I have always considered one of the greatest graces of my life; for at that age I was not favored with lights from heaven as I am now."

This grace she received was the knowledge that she would become a great saint, and, as she is writing, some fourteen years later, she repeats that she is still sure, and feels the same daring confidence, that she will become a *great saint*. The italics are hers. "Our Lord made me understand that the only true glory is the glory which lasts forever; and that to attain it there is no necessity to do brilliant deeds; rather should we hide our good works from the eyes of others, and even from ourselves, so that 'the left hand knows not what the right hand does.' Then, as I reflected that I was born for great things, and sought the means to attain them, it was made known to me interiorly that my personal glory would never reveal itself before the eyes of men, but would consist in becoming a saint."

And it is true that when she lay dying, she overheard one of the other sisters saying, "It will be hard to find something to write about the life of Therese to send around to the other Carmels," so hidden and uneventful was her life outwardly.

For a time, too, she was ambitious for knowledge. "I had always loved everything noble and beautiful and now I had a great thirst for knowledge; not satisfied with what my governess was teaching me, I began to study other subjects by myself, and learnt more in a few months than I had ever done at school, though this zeal was probably just 'vanity and vexation of spirit.' As I was so impetuous this was a very dangerous moment in my life. . . ."

Her great love at this period was the *Imitation of Christ*, "because I had not yet discovered the hidden treasures of the Gospels. Much to everybody's amusement, I always used to have it with me and my aunt would often open it at random and make me say by heart the first chapter she came to."

Later on she came across what she called "the honey and oil" of the conferences of one Father Arminjon: a work called *The End of this World and the Mysteries of the World to Come*. Although Father Arminjon's book would not seem to be an attractive subject for a child to be pondering over, these meditations gave her the long view, a sense of perspective, a realization of the fleetingness of life and the greatness of man's destiny, which she never forgot. "As I read I experienced that joy which the world cannot give, something of what God has prepared for those who love Him."

It was later, during her convent life, that she read all of St. John of the Cross and the works of St. Teresa of Avila. She was still in her teens when she read these great masterpieces of the spiritual life, the work of two of the greatest mystics the world has known. Later she was to say that she could read nothing but the Gospels, and was so nourished by them, she so loved them, that she wore them under her clothes, next to her heart.

On another page of her autobiography she refers to Surin's *Foundations of the Spiritual Life*. Aside from these references, all her quotations are from the Scriptures, and in all there are one hundred and thirty of them from both the Old and the New Testaments. During these last few years of her life, the Bible was her only reading.

XI

Mental Illness

THE ILLNESSES from which Therese suffered in childhood—
the only illnesses she mentions in her story—were mental
ones. When she was nine years old, and Pauline left the home
at Les Buissonnets for Carmel, Therese began to be afflicted
with a mysterious illness, which began with severe headaches.
She went on to school just the same and continued her studies
all during the fall of 1882. But "my heart was torn with
grief . . . and I said from the depths of my heart, 'Pauline is
lost to me.' "

Her headaches were bearable, she said, though she felt herself to be seriously ill. Evidently not too much attention was
paid to her illness, however, for Mr. Martin went to Paris
with Marie and Leonie around Easter time, 1883, leaving
Celine and Therese with their aunt and uncle and cousins.

One evening when she was alone with her uncle Isidore, he
began to talk to her very seriously about her mother and the
time when he was a little boy, and Therese began to cry. He
was touched at her sensitiveness, she writes, and determined
to do all he could to distract her and her sister during the
vacations. But that very evening her headaches became acute
and she was seized with a strange shivering which lasted all
night. "My aunt, like a real mother never left me for a moment; all through my illness she lavished on me the most
tender and devoted care. You may imagine my poor Father's
grief when he returned from Paris to find me in this hopeless

state; he thought I was going to die, but our Lord might have said to him: 'This sickness is not unto death, but for the glory of God.' "

Then began a period of careful and ceaseless nursing, with Marie and Leonie constantly at her side. They tried to avoid mentioning the clothing day of Pauline, which was approaching, thinking that Therese would be too sick to go; in her own heart, however, she knew that she would go. And so it turned out. She was able to leave her bed, rejoice with her sister, admire her beautiful bridal clothing, hide under her veil, and the hour was one of great happiness. She felt well all that day, but the next morning she had a relapse, and "became so ill, that humanly speaking, there was no hope of her recovery."

I do not know how to describe this extraordinary illness [she wrote], I said things which I had never thought of; I acted as though I were forced to act in spite of myself; I seemed nearly always to be delirious; and yet I feel certain that I was never, for a minute, deprived of my reason. Sometimes I remained in a state of extreme exhaustion for two hours together, unable to make the least movement, and yet, in spite of this extraordinary torpor, hearing the least whisper. I remember it still. And what fears the devil inspired! I was afraid of everything. My bed seemed to be surrounded by frightful precipices; nails in the wall took the terrifying appearance of long fingers, shrivelled and blackened with fire, making me cry out in terror. One day, while Papa stood looking at me in silence, the hat in his hand was suddenly transformed into some horrible shape, and I was so frightened that he went away sobbing.

But if God allowed the devil to approach me in this open way, Angels too were sent to console and strengthen me. Marie never left me, and never showed the least trace of weariness in spite of all the trouble I gave her—for I could not rest while she was away. During meals when Victoire took care of me, I never ceased calling tearfully "Marie, Marie!" When she was going out, it was only if she were going to Mass or to see Pauline that I kept quiet. As for Leonie, and my little Celine, they could not do enough for me. On Sundays they shut themselves up for hours with a poor child who seemed almost to have lost her reason. My own dear sisters, how much I made you suffer! My aunt came to see me every day and brought me many little gifts. I could never tell you how my love for these dear ones increased during this illness. I understood better than ever what Papa had so often told us: "Always remember, children, that your uncle and aunt have devoted themselves to you in a way that is quite exceptional." In his old age, he experienced this himself, and now he must bless and protect those who lavished on him such affectionate care.

(The aunt, Mme. Guerin, died in 1900 at the age of 55, a few years after the Little Flower. She was thirty-eight when she was paying these visits to her niece, so we can think of her still as young and fresh. The mother herself of two little girls, she must have felt very tenderly about Therese. The uncle died in 1909, a beautiful death, the translator of the *Life* of the Little Flower, T. N. Taylor, notes. Therese made her presence felt several times before her aunt's death, "assisting her in an extraordinary way.")

"When my sufferings grew less," the story continues, "my delight was to weave garlands of daisies and forget-me-nots for our Lady's statue. We were in the beautiful month of May, when all nature is clothed with the flowers of spring; the Little Flower alone drooped, and seemed as though it had withered forever."

This illness was an interruption in her early school years. Celine, on the other hand missed only two days in six years.

Therese had been sick now since the previous October, though it was not until Easter that her sickness grew so acute that the family thought she was dying. Until then it had been a matter of constant headaches. By May, however, she had grown so much worse that her father sent an offering to the shrine of Our Lady of Victories in Paris asking that a novena of Masses be offered to obtain the cure of his youngest child. This little church had become famous around 1836. A saintly priest, Abbé Desgenettes had started a confraternity of the

Immaculate Heart of Mary there for the conversion of sinners.

And a miracle, according to Therese, was wrought by Our Lady of Victories herself.

One Sunday during the Novena Marie went into the garden, leaving me with Leonie who was reading by the window. After a short time I began to call: "Marie! Marie!" very softly. Leonie, accustomed to hearing me fret like this, took no notice, so I called louder until Marie came back to me. I saw her come into the room quite well, but for the first time, I failed to recognize her. I looked all around and glanced anxiously into the garden, still calling: "Marie! Marie!" Her anguish was perhaps greater than mine, and that was unutterable. At last, after many fruitless efforts to make me recognize her, she whispered a few words to Leonie, and went away pale and trembling. Leonie carried me to the window. [She must have wasted away, this child of ten.] There I saw the garden with Marie walking up and down, but still I did not recognize her; she came forward smiling and held out her arms to me, calling tenderly: "Therese, dear little Therese!" This last effort failing, she came in again and knelt in tears at the foot of my bed; turning to the statue of Our Lady, she entreated her with the fervor of a mother who begs the life of her child and will not be refused. Leonie and Celine joined her, and that cry of faith forced the gates of heaven. I, too, finding no help on earth and nearly dead with pain, turned to my heavenly Mother begging her from the bottom of my heart to have pity on me. Suddenly the statue came to life and grew beautiful with a divine beauty that I shall never find words to describe. The expression on Our Lady's face was ineffably sweet, tender and compassionate; but what touched me to the very depths of my soul was her gracious smile. Then all my pain vanished, two big tears started to my eyes and fell silently. . . .

They were indeed tears of unmixed heavenly joy. "Our blessed Lady has come to me, she has smiled at me. How happy I am, but I shall tell no one, or my happiness will leave me!" Such were my thoughts. Looking round, I recognized Marie; she seemed very much overcome, and looked lovingly at me, as though she guessed that I had just received a great grace.

Indeed her prayers had gained me this unspeakable favor, a smile from the blessed Virgin! When she saw me with my eyes fixed on the statue, she said to herself, "Therese is cured!" And it was true. The Little Flower had come to life again—a bright ray from its glorious sun had warmed and set it free forever from its cruel enemy. "The dark winter is past, the rain is over and gone," and Our Lady's Little Flower gathered such strength that five years later it opened wide its petals on the fertile mountains of Carmel.

Therese was deprived of all joy in this experience because in her gratitude she told it to her sister Marie, to whom she gave a reluctant permission to repeat it to the Sisters at Carmel. The Sisters asked her so many questions, and her answers satisfied them so little—how put into words such an experience—that she "began to persuade herself she had been guilty of an untruth" and she "looked on herself with feelings of contempt." Strong words for a ten-year-old child to use toward herself.

If one can call hypersensitiveness or scruples an illness, then there was another crisis for her to pass through also.

It was during her retreat before her second Holy Communion that she "fell a prey to scruples and I remained in this unhappy state for nearly two years. It is not possible for me to describe all the sufferings it entailed; one must have passed through such a martyrdom to be able to understand it. Every thought, every action, even the simplest, was a source of trouble and anguish; no peace came to me till I told everything to Marie, and that cost me a great deal, for I imagined myself obliged to lay open absolutely all my thoughts, even the most extravagant. This done, I experienced a momentary peace, but it passed like a flash and once again the martyrdom began."

She had a headache nearly every day of this time, and

when she tried to get some sympathy for it, both her cousin and her aunt reproached her and felt she was concealing something from them, some scruple which she would not tell. Evidently she confided only in Marie, and since they saw she got no better, they may have thought they themselves could help her more.

Scruples made her so ill, she said, that she had to be taken from school when she was thirteen. To complete her education, her father had her tutored several days a week, and she came more into contact with the outside world. This was the period when she overheard much, "even of what it would have been far better I should not hear." And I suppose she meant other things than the flattering remarks visitors made about her beauty.

To help herself she joined the sodality of the Children of Mary and went twice a week to the Benedictine Convent, where she had attended school, to take part in a sewing class, but still she had no friends and found all conversation with others wearisome. She felt the indifference of others keenly, after the warmth of her home.

At this time Marie, who was then twenty-six, entered the Carmel where Pauline had entered some years before, and Therese shed more tears.

But tears at that time were nothing unusual; they flowed for the most trivial cause. I was most anxious, for instance, to advance in virtue, yet I went about it in a strange way. I had never been accustomed to wait on myself, nor do any housework, and Celine always arranged our room. Now, however, with the intention of pleasing our Lord, I would sometimes make my bed, or if Celine happened to be out, I would bring in her plants and cuttings. Since it was for Our Lord's sake that I did these little things I ought not to have looked for any return. But, alas! I did look for thanks, and if, unfortunately, Celine did not seem surprised and grateful for my small services, I was disappointed, as my tears soon showed. Again, if I unintentionally offended anyone, far from making the best of it, I fretted until I became quite ill, thus increasing my fault instead of repairing it. Then when I began to be reconciled to the blunder, I would cry for having cried. In fact, I made troubles out of everything.

Therese's account of the nervous, neurotic state she was in for almost two years does not take many pages, nor does the story of her illness at the departure of Pauline. Both of these illnesses, scruples as well as the former mysterious ailment, would be considered today to be some form of mental or nervous breakdown, and certainly such patients do not receive the sympathy they feel they need, nor the understanding. In later years, when one of the nuns in the convent was considered to be a neurasthenic, Therese remarked to her sister, "How gladly would I have been Infirmarian to take care of that sister. Grace would have spoken louder than nature. Yes, I have a taste for that work. And with how much love I would have done it. Oh, how I should have made that sister happy, especially in calling to mind those words of Jesus: 'I was sick and you visited me.' "

She would have made her happy, she said! In other words she would have listened, as Marie listened to her, as Celine listened, as her father listened. She would have treated that poor soul delicately, with consideration, with patience, even for two years, as she had been treated. Or forever. I am sure we should pray to St. Therese about those around us who are going through this suffering, these "nervous breakdowns," these delusions. If her "way" is for all, surely we should recognize her experience, and her desire to help in this field, too.

The state she was in passed as abruptly as it had come upon her. Her older sister on whom she leaned had left her for the convent (another example of the ruthless search for God, this unquestioning obedience to the call of God, this clear, pure recognition of God's will).

She had Celine still and they were all but inseparable. But it was through the intervention of her little dead brothers in heaven that she suddenly received the grace to "snap out of it," to use the expressive slang of our day. It was as sudden as that. They had come in from midnight Mass, the father and three daughters, Leonie, Celine and Therese. Therese, now fourteen years old, had put out her shoes for presents by the open fireplace in the living room. After the glory of the religious observance and the spiritual feast, what seemed to be a frivolous clinging to childish things struck the father's eye on their return. He said with some "crossness" (Therese's own word for it), "Therese ought to have outgrown all this sort of thing, and I hope this will be the last time."

Therese was on the stairs on her way to her room to take off her things, and Celine, ever her comforter, whispered to her not to go downstairs right away for fear their father would see how hurt she was. "Don't go down just yet; you'll only go and cry if you open your presents now in front of father."

But Therese said she was not the same Therese any more. In the twinkling of an eye she had been given that strength and control which she had so lacked these last years. "I have been happy ever since," she wrote.

On that night she opened her presents gaily, though she confessed her heart was beating fast, and she said that she looked as happy as a queen; her father too, no longer cross, entered into the fun of it. A great change had taken place. "Therese had once for all regained the strength of mind which had left her when she was four and a half.

"On this radiant night began the third period of my life, the most beautiful of all, the most filled with heavenly favors. Satisfied with my good will, Our Lord accomplished in an instant the work I had not been able to do during years. Love and a spirit of self-forgetfulness took complete possession of my heart, and thenceforward I was perfectly happy."

Therese calls this a "conversion" and regards this cure as a turning point in her life. The first period was that of her childhood, up to the time of her mother's death when Therese was almost five. The second period ended when she was within a week of her fourteenth birthday. Altogether she had experienced five years of acute mental and physical suffering, with some flashes of great peace and even of ecstasy.

XII

Vocation

A VOCATION, as the word is commonly used by Catholics, is a desire for the religious life, a call usually as definite as the call of our Lord in those days when He began numbering his Apostles or when He told the rich young man to sell all he had, give to the poor and come and follow Him. St. Thomas wrote that if one had this call one should run to it. But Dom Chapman, the great Benedictine spiritual advisor of recent years, urges his penitents to wait, to try in every way to get out of it, and only when the call becomes most insistent, to follow it. "Many are called, but few are chosen" is generally interpreted to mean that many are called just as Therese's mother and father felt themselves to be, though they were destined not for that particular way of life but for the married state. Many are not even called to that, but to the life of the celibate in the world, a difficult vocation too.

The parents of the Little Flower had been happy in their vocation and, from the way they wrote to each other, they very definitely did not feel that they were choosing the second best. They had accepted the rulings of the monastery and convent where they had applied for admission as the will of God, and then waited until circumstances would show them what was the further will of their Creator.

The love they both had for the children they were bringing into the world, the feeling they had of being co-creators with God, their sense of fulfilment, their joy at adding to the sum total of praise of God in the world, all this is expressed in the story of their lives.

The Normans are a sturdy and hardy people with their feet firmly planted on the good rich soil of the countryside, and Louis and Zelie were whole man and woman, with a proper balance of soul and body, and to them the marriage act was as truly a sacrament as Holy Orders.

They had longed for a son to be a priest but God had sent them two little boys only to take them back again, and had then, instead, inspired the five daughters who remained to them to enter the religious state. When Zelie died, she did not know how any of them were going to grow up, though she was quite sure that Pauline was going to be a nun.

When Louis Martin was told by Pauline and Marie that they were going to enter Carmel, he wept at losing them, but was glad nevertheless. He knew their firm spirits, and he knew that they would be happy. He knew they would persevere, no matter if on occasion, as sometimes happens, they might doubt their vocation. They would hold fast, as they would have held fast to a marriage, through sickness and health, till death, and through death, since they chose Christ, since they had been called by Christ their Spouse, their Brother.

Therese too had always said that she was going to be a nun. If Pauline was a nun, then she too would be a nun, and she had confided this desire to Mother Marie de Gonzague, the Superior of the Carmel where her two sisters were.

It was on Christmas, 1886, that Therese had suddenly been cured of her sensitiveness, her weeping. It was so important a date in her life that she always called it her conversion. Certainly she had prayed, all during those two years when she suffered agonies of self-consciousness and of guilt. She had prayed to be relieved of her mental torture—she herself termed it torture—but there had seemingly been no result. She did not improve little by little. Her cure happened at once on that momentous Christmas eve.

One need only to read such spiritual writers as Father

Faber and his conferences on Self Deceit and Hurt Feelings
to realize how sore an affliction this was that Therese had
suffered. Father Faber has emphasized these failings from
the standpoint of pride and lack of charity, almost as though
those who suffered from these spiritual states were imputing
to others meanings and moods never intended by them. But
in the brief handling of this period in Therese's story, and in
the writings of her sisters about her childhood, the deposi-
tions taken at her canonization proceedings, there is quite
another emphasis. More than in any spiritual writer, save
perhaps St. Francis de Sales, the emphasis is on naked, blind
charity. This difficult spiritual and mental state was an ailment, and was treated as such by the family, with tenderness
and consideration and infinite patience. The sisters of St.
Therese never saw any fault in her, any deliberate selfishness,
self-centeredness, any lack of charity towards others. Marie
had handled her sister's case until her own rather sudden
vocation called her to Carmel, and then it was Celine who
was the patient companion.

After her "conversion," Therese and Celine were more
than ever close to each other and they spent hours together,
reading and speaking about God. "We had found already the
One we were seeking and 'when we were alone He gave us
His kiss, and now no one may despise us.' "

Celine was Therese's confidante, not the confessor she went
to at the parish church, though she wrote later that she would
act differently in the light of later knowledge. She went to
Communion as often as her confessor allowed her, but she
did not tell him of her longing to go each day. She said that,
because she was so conscious of the great favors and graces
she received, she thought that in her case, Jesus acted directly on her soul, and not through a director.

She kept silence as far as priests and nuns were concerned,
for in telling about one divine favor—the sight of the statue
of the Blessed Virgin coming to life—she had brought upon
herself such unhappiness that she later wondered if she had
been deceived.

In Therese's world, she was faced with only three choices. She could look forward to marriage, or to living at home as a single woman and caring for her father, or to entering the convent. The atmosphere of this home was one of such liberty that the girls were always free to decide what they wanted, what they themselves thought was God's will for them. Marie, the oldest, "I-am-quite-free Marie," had stayed away from the convent until she was twenty-six years old. Pauline had already been there five years. With two sisters now in the Carmel in Lisieux it was natural that Therese should turn to Carmel. Leonie, the third oldest sister, later went to the Visitation convent, and if she had chosen Carmel, it is doubtful whether a fifth sister would have been permitted to enter, after Celine had joined the others. After all, a Carmelite convent has no more than twenty-one nuns, and the older St. Teresa, the reformer, preferred the number to be kept down to twelve or thirteen.

This way in which Therese had now set her feet led to Carmel, where Pauline was the only one of her sisters to encourage her when she confided that she wished to enter. Marie thought she was too young and, considering the difficulties Marie had undergone not so long since with her little sister, her conclusion was only natural. Marie had not been living with Therese at Christmas time when her way of thinking and acting had undergone an amazingly sudden change. Probably Mother Marie de Gonzague was no longer encouraging now that the time had arrived for a decision to be made.

Therese already had two sisters in Carmel, and Celine also wished to enter. Since she was the elder, by rights she should have entered first, but when she discovered what Therese wanted to do, she nobly stepped aside and agreed to stay at home for a while longer. If Therese went first to the convent, that meant that Celine had to care for the father who had suffered a serious attack of paralysis that year from which, however, he had rather quickly recovered. Leonie had already tried one convent and planned to try her vocation once more. Even now, late as this, the girls did not seem to depend on Leonie as they did on each other.

Some months after that famous Christmas, on the feast of Pentecost, Therese told her father of her desires. She did it in fear and trembling, at the close of the day, after they had come home from Vespers. Her father was sitting in the garden; it was sunset at the end of a most beautiful day. She had prayed to the Holy Spirit and to the Apostles to help her to speak, to ask her father's permission. After all, she was only fourteen.

The very words she uses in her autobiography show how important she considered her vocation, how out of the ordinary, not in the least like that of others. She felt herself to be, she wrote, "a child destined by God to be, by means of prayer and sacrifice, an apostle of apostles." Already once before, when out walking with her father, she had pointed to the large T made by the configuration of the stars and said childishly, "Look, my name is written in heaven." She felt her vocation to be a saint—and a special kind of a saint for our times.

When she told her father he wept at first. He tried to tell her she was too young to leave him, to take such a step into a harsh and rigorous life. But they continued to talk as they walked up and down the garden path, and her heart grew light with joy when she realized that he had consented. After they had walked for some time together, he stooped down to a little rock garden and picked a small white flower, which came out by the roots. Then he spoke to her of her sheltered life, and how God had chosen her, a little flower, preserving her in her fragility and obscurity. From then on she thought of herself as "a little white flower"—the name she first gave to her book. She took the flower and pressed it in her prayer book and since the roots had come up with the stem, she thought of herself as being transplanted to Carmel. Later, when the stem broke, she took it as a sign that she was going to die young, as she did.

Her uncle, too, was won over within a week although at

first he vehemently opposed her entrance. He was a legal guardian by her mother's wishes and he had a right to speak. He said that it was against human prudence for a child of her age to enter so strict an order and that religion would be greatly harmed if she were allowed to do so. There was enough criticism of religion in those days.

Between the time of her uncle's first objection and his acceptance of the idea, Therese was in a state of deep dejection that lasted for three days and which she compared to the time the child Jesus was lost. She said she understood what Mary and Joseph had suffered. It was as though she were lost in some frightful desert. "There was only night, dark night, utter desolation like death itself." She does not hesitate to go on and compare this time to the agony in the garden and she said that she felt forsaken, with no consolation on earth or in heaven. Months of joy and strength, and then again a feeling of powerlessness. Her life seems full of such contrasts, such vehement moods.

When her uncle had been won over, news came from Pauline that Canon Delatroette, the Superior of Carmel, would not allow Therese to enter until she was twenty-one. Almost six more long years! One must remember how long the days are in childhood, how long the months, how interminable the years.

Then began a round of visits that were to take her to Rome itself, to the feet of the Holy Father, Leo XIII.

Pauline had given her the bad news, and she courageously went with her father to the home of the Superior, who treated her coldly and said that nothing would make him change his mind. But later he added that he was only the Bishop's delegate; if the Bishop were to allow her to enter he, the Superior, could not stand in her way. With this door opened, Mr. Martin offered to take her to Bayeux where the Bishop lived, and although she looked forward to this adventure, it could not be arranged at once.

Meanwhile, many other things happened. There was a holiday at the seashore and Leonie went to the convent again.

Therese's life of work and study continued and she felt herself growing in the love of God. It is here that she speaks of experiencing "transports of love." Over and over again in books on St. Therese, it is emphasized that her way is a most ordinary way, a way open to all. She herself says that it was her destiny to show the world of today that holiness is accessible to all, that all are called, and that it is a "little way," a simple way for all to follow. And never once does she say that these transports, these joys are not for all. As well as the Cross, there are the joys of the spiritual life. Little attention has been paid to these joys in the life of Therese.

In spite of the delays that tormented her she speaks of these days as of a time when she was in love and growing in love and when she thought of hell as a place where love is not. She wished to go to that place of blasphemy and torment so that even there God could be loved eternally. "When one is in love one says so many foolish things," she adds. Heaven meant nothing to her save love.

One of the delays that summer was caused by the illness of a poor acquaintance, and it became Therese's job to care for the woman's two little children, both of them under six. This task was just one of the many activities of a family which was always full of charity and help for the poor.

The older St. Teresa, of Avila, tells of a "conversion" experienced on having a vision of our Lord's humanity. St. Therese had some such experience when, one Sunday after Mass, a picture of the crucifixion slipped partly out of her missal, showing the Divine Hands, pierced and bleeding. "An indescribable thrill, such as I had never before experienced, passed through me; my heart was torn with grief."

From then on she felt a desire to satisfy the thirst of Christ for souls, and the thought that people did not realize the price the God-Man had paid tortured her. Therese wanted to save souls, and she started with confidence by working (in her prayers) on a notorious criminal just about to go to the guillotine. Pranzini (no other name is ever given him) was born in Alexandria, Egypt, and brought up a good Catholic. He was well educated and could speak eight languages, so that he was able to obtain work as an interpreter. He lived a dissolute life, however, and landed in France utterly destitute. After finding work in Paris, he murdered three people, one of them a child of eleven. He was tracked to Marseilles and arrested just as he was about to take the boat for Alexandria. Tried and found guilty, he spent his time in prison translating "bad books into different languages." He always denied his crime and only consented to see the chaplain "to get tobacco and to while away the time."

The execution took place at dawn on August 31, 1887, and, as usual at that time, a huge crowd—some thirty thousand—assembled outside the prison to see the death sentence carried out. A description of such a public execution in Paris is given in *An Old Wive's Tale* by Arnold Bennett, and no doubt the newspapers at the time were full of the details of the horror.

Therese felt herself "lifted out of the narrow sphere in which she lived," capable of tremendous things, of asking the greatest favors of God, now that she was cured of scruples. She asked for the conversion of this murderer who had refused to see a priest.

My God [she prayed], I am sure Thou wilt pardon this unhappy Pranzini, and I shall still think so even if he does not confess his sins or give any sign of sorrow—such is the confidence I have in Thy unbounded mercy. But because this is my first sinner, I beg for just one sign of repentance to reassure me.

My prayer was granted to the letter. Though Papa never allowed us to read newspapers, I did not consider it an act of disobedience when, on the day following the execution, I hastily opened the paper, *La Croix,* and looked for the part concerning Pranzini. What was it I saw? Tears betrayed my emotion and I was forced to run from the room. Without confession or absolution Pranzini had mounted the scaffold, and the executioners were dragging him towards the fatal block, when all at once, apparently in answer to a sudden inspiration, he turned round, seized a crucifix which the priest held towards him, *and kissed Our Lord's Sacred Wounds three times.* . . .

The lips of my first born had been pressed to those Divine Wounds.

She felt that her apostolate of saving souls had begun.

She tells this story in the beginning of the chapter about her vocation, and although she has always said that she intended to be a nun, one might say that her thirst for souls and for saving sinners intensified this desire.

Therese visited Carmel often and talked over her desires with her sisters and also with the Prioress. It speaks well for the discernment of the Prioress, that she recognized from the first the vocation of this fourteen-year-old child who had been visiting there since she was eight.

Even with two sisters in Carmel, it is not likely that St. Therese knew all of the troubles of the convent as they were afterwards revealed. But even if she had known—and perhaps she discerned the character of her future Prioress more clearly than people think—it would have made no difference, I am sure, because Therese was entering Carmel to do penance and to save souls. All had not been harmony in her own home, with Leonie often harsh and difficult, a servant cruel and secretive, her own early breakdown, and the scruples that afterward tormented her. She had gone through suffering already, even though to read her story as she wrote it one would think of her life as one of complete harmony and peace. There was much natural happiness, yes, of family and relatives, but there was also sickness and death, there were all the little trials of community living, besides the big trials that the child had already gone through. After what she called her "conversion" she felt strong and ready for anything, even to imprisoning herself, immuring herself, as the saying is, within a poor, cramped convent, unheated in the cold Normandy winters, with twenty or so other women of all ages, young postulants, and old, crippled and senile nuns.

She who begged God always to let her see the truth, not to

deceive herself, surely she must have known the character of the Prioress. And how she loved her!

Mother Marie de Gonzague was an aristocrat, perhaps a rather petty one, since she seemed to set some store on her birth. One of the complaints made against her was that she did not leave her family behind when she entered the convent, and that even within the walls the nuns were forced as part of their work to embroider fine linens for her relatives. Some authors make quite a point of this family situation. But Therese in her short autobiography never refers to it. The Prioress is described as harsh and moody, and of course an inkling of this is given. After the child had entered the convent finally, there was never a day during her time as postulant on which she was not scolded on one pretext or another. Her vocation was indeed tried.

Mother Marie is supposed to have had a cat of which she was very fond and which was the cause of some of the complaints made against her. One night, after Compline, when the Great Silence began, she herself broke the strictly kept silence and ordered the nuns to break it because the cat had been lost. Another complaint was that, on one occasion when the cat caught a bird, the nun who was doing the cooking was ordered to roast it and serve it to her majesty the cat!

There seems to be a lot of pettiness in these complaints, and what person in authority has not been subject to such criticisms?

At any rate, St. Therese says herself that when, at the age of nine, she told the Prioress of her wish to become a nun like her sister Pauline, she was encouraged in her desire. I suppose the family visited the convent to see Pauline as often as they were allowed, and relatives of the nuns were allowed to talk face-to-face with their loved ones. That is, the black curtain that hung suspended behind the iron or wooden bars, which separated visitors from the nuns, was withdrawn. In the Visitation convents, in the cloistered Dominicans, there is no black curtain, and those same bars may be a decorative wooden screen symbolizing the separation of the nun from the world in her enclosure. In the Carmelite convents, the separation seems severe.

I will always remember the first time I visited a Carmel, which was housed in an old mansion in Newport, Rhode Island. The Mother Superior had written me often and on the occasion of my visit she was very glad to see me, but there was no relaxing of the rules. I could enter a parlor for visitors, pray in the big chapel—the main part of which is reserved for the public—but I could not see the nuns in their side chapel, which was like an arm of the cross and heavily screened, nor could I see the Mother Superior in the little parlor. There was a heavy black curtain between us, and I had the illusion that she could see me, but that I could not see her, which was embarrassing. To give or to receive anything from the nuns—food, books, or clothing—one had to use a turnstile like a revolving doorway, built in the wall. The physical separation certainly emphasized the dedication of these women to a life of prayer and penance.

However much or little Therese knew about life inside the Lisieux Carmel, one thing is certain. She knew that her vocation lay within its walls and that she must take every means to enter as soon as possible.

It was not until October that there was a chance to visit the Bishop in Bayeux and to make the request that an exception be made to the rule of not accepting a postulant at Carmel until she was twenty-one.

The date of the visit had been set by the Vicar General, Father Reverony, who met Therese and her father and escorted them to the vast parlor of the Bishop's palace—a room with huge armchairs before the fire. Telling them to take a seat, Father Reverony directed Therese to a huge chair while he turned to a little one. When she demurred, he told her sharply to show that she could obey. When the Bishop entered, Therese and her father knelt to kiss his ring. She had expected her father to open the conversation, but he motioned her to tell the object of their visit. She spoke ardently of her desire to enter Carmel, feeling all but hopeless as she spoke. When the Bishop asked her how long she had been wanting to become a Carmelite, she told him that she had entertained the wish for a very long time. The two clergymen laughed at her youth, and her father joined in, saying that it was only that day that she had put her golden curls up on her head to look older than she was.

The Bishop tried to make her see that it was her duty to stay with her father a while longer, but her father stated that he was perfectly willing to give her up. He added that, since he and Therese were going to join the diocesan pilgrimage to Rome, they would not hesitate to speak to the Holy Father himself.

The Bishop kindly promised to speak to the Superior at Lisieux and to forward the answer to Rome at once so she would have no delay.

It was three days after this pilgrimage to Bayeux that the Martins started on the trip to Rome, the father and the only two members of his family then left at home—Celine and Therese. Leonie was at the Visitation convent in Caen on another of her early unsuccessful attempts at religious life.

XIII

Pilgrimage

AT THAT TIME there was tension between Church and State. There were demonstrations in Italy, looting of convents. In France pilgrimages were looked upon as monarchist demonstrations as well as religious observances. Unfortunately, as so often happens, the well-to-do, the aristocrat, was equated in the popular mind with the monarchist, the reactionary, and with the Church. The nobility of the diocese in which the Martins lived were either showing courage in demonstrating by a great pilgrimage their loyalty to the Church and the Holy See or were displaying an arrogant disregard of the temper of the times. Who can judge? Certainly the Martin family did not set itself up to judge. Mr. Martin went on the pilgrimage because he could afford it, and because he wanted his Therese and Celine to have an audience with the Pope. Therese was determined to speak out and ask permission to enter Carmel, young as she was.

It was a journey which only confirmed Therese's determination to leave the world.

Yes, all the nobility of the diocese were going on that pilgrimage; in fact, it seemed to be made up only of them, "but we were not impressed," Therese said simply. The Martin family had come up against this sort of thing before. Their aunt, Sister Marie Dosithea, had spent her life as a nun with an order long associated with the aristocracy. During her school days at the Visitation convent, Marie had been tempted to emulate her friends there, but her father had teased her out of her affectations.

They were an exclusive family in quite another way. Louis and Zelie Martin were both workers, both used to manual labor. He was a shopkeeper—a member of a class that was looked down upon not only by the wealthy and noble, but even by the Church. The Martins were neither peasants, close to real things and the life of the soil, nor were they rich. Louis Martin was able to retire only because they had lived in great frugality. Only when the children were young did they have chocolate for early breakfast. When they got older it was onion soup. Coffee appeared at the main meal only on great feasts. Aside from visiting the Guerin family and receiving visits from them, and perhaps from friends, there is more often an account of the Martins receiving into their home the poor—rather than the well-born—to sit at their table and join in their feasts.

That there was quite a consciousness in the family of this difference in rank is brought out by Therese in her autobiography and by others who have written about the pilgrimage to Rome. Always there was a consciousness of their dignity as children of the Great King and Therese's pride in her father's unusual holiness, which shone out to the others as well.

"Although they had no handle to their name," Father Piat writes, "they formed such an attractive trio, and had something so disinterested about them that the hotel servants made mistakes at times and were particular to show them marked respect."

One does not spend some weeks in the company of a large group of people without knowing them pretty well and seeing their faults. Travel is hard and pilgrimages are harder. To while away the long hours in the train some of the pilgrims played cards and wanted the girls to join them, but Mr. Martin suggested amiably that it was, after all, a pilgrimage. On such an occasion one of the pilgrims did not hesitate to show his scorn.

"Presently their annoyance became evident," Therese writes, "and then dear Papa began quietly to defend us, pointing out that as we were on a pilgrimage more of our time might be given to prayer. One of the players, forgetting the respect due to age, called out thoughtlessly: Thank God, pharisees are rare! My father did not answer a word, he even seemed pleased; and later on he found an opportunity of shaking hands with this man, and speaking so pleasantly that the latter must have thought that his rude words had either not been heard, or at least were forgotten."

Mr. Martin had always loved travel and had taken long trips all over Europe. But this was the first long trip for the two girls, Celine who was seventeen, and Therese fourteen. They were both lively and in Milan climbed the 484 steps to the roof of the Duomo, went down among the ruins in the Colosseum in Rome, up and down through the Catacombs, where they were present at Mass and where they lay in the crypt where St. Cecilia's body had been found.

Therese had never had any particular knowledge or devotion to this little saint, but now she began to have a "love of friendship" for her. She made St. Cecilia her patroness. It was not because she was a patroness of musicians, but because she sang in her heart during trials and had unbounded confidence "enabling her to purify souls who had never desired anything but the joys of the world." Later in her life Therese began to wear the Gospels next to her heart because it is said of St. Cecilia: "the Holy Gospels lay ever on her breast."

She not only showed no fatigue, she was fearless. On one occasion, a group of demonstrating students seized upon the pilgrims and lifted Therese, the youngest of them, aloft, carrying her on their shoulders. It must have been a startling and disconcerting experience. "Even a friendly mob has the smell of the beast," someone has said, and at a time in history of anticlerical riots, this incident was a reminder to Therese. She was learning many things not in the guide books.

Another time, on the hairpin curves of the drives around

Sorrento, a horse ran away with the carriage she was in. One
can imagine the terror of such an experience. Still another
time she got lost—separated from her party because she had
lost her belt buckle and had gone back to the cathedral to
search for it. Coming back to the carriages, the only one she
found there was that of the clergy and she had to accept a
seat with those whom she knew thought her entry into a
Carmel a childish dream.

Therese was attractive enough to draw attention, everyone
remarked on her beauty and her bright golden hair. One man,
on the occasion of her canonization, said that he used to sit
behind her in church just to see that cascade of golden curls.

One of the notable things about Therese, this little modern
saint, was the physical expression of her joys and sorrows
and desires. If she wanted to express love, she did so in no
uncertain terms, and her unbounded enthusiasm, her vitality
on this expedition must have made her a joy as a companion.
She seems to have suffered no fatigue, though they took in
all the sights and visited every holy place. When their father
was tired he let another family take charge of his daughters.
After their arrival at Rome, they had six days of sight-seeing
and then on Sunday morning, November 20, they attended
the Mass of the Holy Father, Pope Leo XIII, at eight o'clock.
After the early Mass there was another one of thanksgiving,
and then the audience with the pilgrims began.

This famous interview during which Therese disobeyed the
Vicar General of her diocese, who forbade anyone to speak,
is usually cited as an example of her courage. Rigid conven-
tion has always been observed at these audiences, and the
members of a pilgrimage were permitted to come forward to
bow their heads to the ground, and to kiss the white slipper
of the seated Pope.

This was the moment that Therese was living for, this was
the time for her to make her request. Father Reverony had
cried out loudly that "he absolutely forbade anyone to speak,"
and with her heart beating wildly, Therese turned to look at

Celine. "Speak," her sister whispered, and the child spoke out bravely: "Most Holy Father, I want to ask a great favor."

The Pope bent his head at once, his face almost touching mine, while his piercing black eyes seemed to be gazing into my soul. I began again: "Most Holy Father, in honor of your Jubilee, let me enter Carmel at fifteen." The Vicar General of Bayeux was startled and far from pleased. "Your Holiness," he interrupted, "this is a child who wishes to enter Carmel; the superiors are already going into the question."

"Very well, my child," said His Holiness, "do what the superiors decide." I clasped my hands and placed them on his knee, while I made the final effort. "Holy Father, if you said yes, everyone else would be willing." He gazed at me steadily, and said, stressing every syllable: "Well, well. You will enter if it is God's will."

As I was about to say more, two of the Noble Guard signed to me to get up, and when they saw that was not enough and that I stayed with my clasped hands upon his knee, they pulled me up, with the help of Father Reverony. As they did so, the Holy Father gently touched my lips with his hand, then lifted it in blessing. His eyes followed me a long way.

She had taken liberties with the Pope himself that she would not have taken with her own father, and she had gone against Church and State, one might say, in disregarding the orders of the Vicar General. One might almost say that she had made a scene, that she had clung to the Holy Father, trying to force him to say yes to her request, so that it had taken two guards and Father Reverony himself to disengage her hands and lift her to her feet. The priest had instructed her once before—at the time of the audience with the Bishop of Bayeux—"to show how she could obey." And here she was disobeying and most publicly too. It was as though she had flaunted public opinion, the authority of the Church. She felt that her mission had failed and her one reason for coming to Rome was gone. She felt that the weather itself changed with her mood, from hopefulness to despair. She wept, and the skies wept too. "It was all over, my journey was to no purpose, its enchantment was at an end."

This is the second time in her life that Therese confesses to what is generally regarded by those in religion as "the sin of disobedience." But there is no question in her mind of sinning. There is only the conviction of the primacy of conscience. Her first exercise of her own judgment in disobeying an order was at the time of the execution of Pranzini, the murderer, when she had read one of the forbidden daily newspapers to find out whether the condemned man had given any sign of repentance before he was put to death.

And here again in the incident with the Pope, she was disobedient. Pauline had told her to speak out. Her father expected her to speak. Celine whispered "Speak!" And she spoke her request.

"It would have been more perfect if she had been obedient," it has been said. "She should have mortified her interior sense of judgment, her understanding and her will, and merely prayed that obstacles would be overcome for her, so that she could enter Carmel." But Therese was eminently a child of common sense. She would use her reason as far as it would take her, and then live by faith, abandoning herself to divine providence. She would work as though all depended on herself, and then pray as though all depended on God, as St. Ignatius advised.

It was not even a case of obeying God rather than man, as St. Peter advised. He said also, "Servants, obey your masters." It was more as though she was obeying her immediate superiors, her father and her two sisters, as well as her own conscience.

The incident also shows her utter trust, her simplicity. Pope Leo XIII, surrounded by grandeur and by respect, regarded as he was as Christ on earth, the head of the Church, did not overawe this child of Normandy. The parent she grew up with was not a mother, but a father. She thought of God as her Father, and went to Him with the same simple trust. When she asked for bread, would he give her a stone? She was to point out later the need we all have for this trust in God's goodness and love for us. If we hide from Him, cower, distrust His mercy, think of Him as unforgiving, what kind of parent-child relationship is that! What crueler hurt could we inflict on Him than this distrust of His love, His mercy?

After the audience with the Pope, there was still sight-seeing to be done. From Rome, the party proceeded to Naples and Pompeii. Therese was awed by the sight of the dense pillar of smoke which even to this day, rises from Vesuvius—a reminder of the terrible tragedy that overtook the city of Pompeii.

During the trip, which lasted a month, they stayed at the best hotels and were surrounded by every luxury, but all the glitter of the world could not still her desire for Carmel. When she looked at the magnificent scenery of Italy and Switzerland, she was glad she was going to have these memories to look back on. "I thought to myself: Later on, in the hour of trial, when enclosed in Carmel, I shall only be able to see a little corner of the sky; I will look back on today and be encouraged; the thought of God's majesty and greatness will put my own small troubles in their place. I will love Him alone, and not make myself unhappy by being taken up with trivialities now that I have caught a glimpse of what He has reserved for those He loves."

"Eye hath not seen, nor ear heard, nor hath it entered into the heart of any man to know what God hath prepared for those that love him." Therese related everything she saw to God and to heaven and could say with St. Catherine of Siena, "All the way to Heaven is Heaven, because He said, I am the Way."

The route back to France was different from the one taken on the way to Rome and the railway ran for miles along by the side of the sea. They went past stormy seas, and sunny seas, and plains rich with orange groves, olives, and palms. They saw the seaports by night all ablaze like fairyland.

Mr. Martin was already planning another pilgrimage, this time to Jerusalem, to distract his child who was so grief-stricken at being refused entrance to Carmel. How great was her hunger, her thirst, how in love she was, longing for those narrow walls, that particular place, that garb, that way of life. She wanted no further traveling, no further quest.

When they arrived home they visited Pauline and Marie at Carmel and told them again—for they had already written letters—about what had happened on the trip. Pauline advised Therese to write again to the Bishop. This she did at once and then settled down to wait for an answer.

How imperious were her demands! She wanted to be able to enter on Christmas day! It was not until New Year's that she received an answer, in the shape of a letter to Mother Marie de Gonzague, authorizing Therese to enter Carmel at once. Mother Marie de Gonzague, however, wanting to have her own say in the matter, once more put off the entry for three months. She very practically thought that a fifteen-year-old girl should not be made to begin her convent life with the rigors of a Lent in Carmel.

At first, Therese says, she did not see why she should add to her sufferings any longer by such a strict life as she had been leading, and she was tempted to give way in little things. "But God made me realize the value of the extra time He gavè me; I made up my mind to more serious mortification than ever. When I say mortification, I do not mean the sort of penance the saints undertake. I was not like those grand souls who practice all kinds of penances from childhood. My mortification consisted in checking my self-will, keeping back an impatient word, doing little things for those around me without their knowing it, and countless things like that."

There were two things the Little Flower learned during her pilgrimage—to disdain the world and to pray for priests. Up to that time, she said, the principal aim of Carmel was unknown to her, a mystery to her. She had seen the need to pray for sinners, to pray for a criminal like the murderer Pranzini. Sinners, yes, because Jesus Christ came to take on Himself the sins of the world, to die for sinners, to lay down His life for His brothers. But for priests, those men who put on Christ, who stand for Christ in the eyes of the faithful and through whose anointed hands we receive the sacraments—those outward and visible signs of grace—that we should have to pray for them with the same heart and fervor with which we pray for sinners was hard for her to realize until she made this pilgrimage.

"I grasped my vocation while I was in Italy, and this alone would have made the journey worth while. I met many saintly priests that month, but I also found out that in spite of being above the angels by their supreme dignity, they were none-the-less men and still subject to human weakness. If holy priests, the salt of the earth as Jesus calls them in the Gospel, need to be prayed for, what about the lukewarm?"

When, during the solemn examination before the profession she was asked her reason for coming to Carmel, she declared: "I have come to save souls and above all to pray for priests."

Again she wrote: "O my Celine, let us live for souls, let us be apostles, especially let us save the souls of priests, souls which should be more transparent than crystal. . . . Alas, how many bad priests there are, how many who are not holy enough. Let us pray, let us suffer for them, and on the last day Jesus will be *grateful*. We shall give Him souls."

To do this work, she knew she had to mount the Cross.

In another letter she says, "Celine *dearest,* it is *always* the same thing I have to say to you; ah! let us pray for priests . . . [The footnote in the volume of her published letters adds that a number of priests in great temptation had just been recommended to the prayers of the Carmelites of Lisieux.] Each day shows how rare are the friends of Jesus. It seems to me that that is what He must feel most . . . ingratitude, especially when He sees souls consecrated to Him giving to others the heart which belongs to Him in so absolute a fashion."

A clear insight into this aspect of her vocation to Carmel was perhaps the principal fruit of the Little Flower's pilgrimage to Rome.

XIV

Carmel

THE CARMELITE CONVENT at Lisieux was founded in March, 1838. Four novices and two professed nuns arrived at Lisieux in a covered wagon, much the same kind of conveyance in which the older St. Teresa of Avila traveled about Spain. They settled in a thatched house where they remained all through the summer. In September, they moved to the site they now occupy. Although this house was larger, it was still very primitive. There was no lack of vocations, but it took the Sisters forty years to accumulate enough money to buy the ground and to build the monastery which was to become Therese's home. When she entered it on April 9, 1888, her sister Pauline had been a member of the community for six years, Marie for one.

One might have thought that she was entering this particular Carmel because she had two sisters there and so that she would not be too far away from her father and her sisters at home. This, of course, would not have been a sufficient reason for the vocation of any of the three sisters who followed Pauline into the community. But there might perhaps have been a particular appeal to all the Martin girls in the missionary spirit which permeated the spiritual life in this convent.

The favorite charity of their mother and father had been the Propagation of the Faith and they had always strongly supported foreign missions. The parents had prayed and hoped for a priest-son who would become a missionary, but had seen their two boys die in infancy.

It was this Lisieux Carmel which, in 1861, had sent four nuns to found the first Carmel in the Far East, at Saigon. The nuns always considered themselves as much missionaries as the priests in the field, joining themselves to them by the spiritual support of their prayer and penance. Later on, when there was question of sending out some nuns to a convent in Hanoi, St. Therese volunteered, but her health was already too badly impaired.

Therese read the life of Father Theophane Venard, now Blessed, and loved him because he continued to remain close in spirit to his family—his father, sister and brother. He wrote letters even from his prison in far-off Indochina. She well understood that love of family. She herself was later urged by her Superior to engage in correspondence with two missionaries she adopted and called her "brothers." The Carmelites of Lisieux considered themselves missionaries, converting the world from their convent cells.

Through her sisters, Therese already knew this particular community of Carmelites, not only in its attractions, but also in the difficulties it might offer. She knew, as we have seen, that she would be putting herself under a Prioress whom others had found difficult and who would play an important part particularly in the first years of her adjustment to convent life.

In a work on the Little Flower which was compiled from the official documents of the Carmel in Lisieux, *Life of The Little Flower,* Monsignor Laveille, Prothonotary Apostolic and Vicar General of Meaux, describes Mother Marie de Gonzague as the daughter of a noble family that had given proof of great initiative and administrative ability. She had enlarged the convent, adding a wing to a building which had been very cramped. "These qualities, joined to a great heart and a charming personality, due in part to careful education in her early years, had no doubt determined the choice of the community.

"But this active and richly endowed nature was not without some defects. Very impressionable, and of somewhat distrustful character, predisposed to melancholy, she did not always possess that even-balanced judgment which makes rule beneficial and inspires subordinates with confidence." And he adds that although she had greatly desired Therese's entrance to the Carmel, the severe treatment with which she began to test her vocation continued even throughout the young nun's last illness.

"Mere Marie de Gonzague confided to me that, in order to exercise Soeur Therese's virtue, she had studiously sought to try her by affecting towards her a certain indifference and severity. She has, moreover, testified to me that this apparently harsh treatment had certainly been very painful to the Servant of God, but that no pain had ever caused her to deviate in the least from perfect obedience." This is the deposition made at the "apostolic process" towards her canonization, by the Abbot of Saint-Michel de Frigolet.

Monsignor Laveille also says, "Certain admittedly brilliant qualities in this Reverend Mother did not conceal the defects in her character nor the imperfections in her government. Our saint's keen intellect perceived those defects even more clearly than did the others, but she understood also how much the Prioress suffered from the silent reproach manifested at times in the attitudes of certain Sisters, and she strove, as did none other, to heal those wounds."

There is no question but that the Carmelite cloister was a fervent one. The very poverty of their lives, the discipline of their days, their sending out nuns to foreign lands to establish new convents proved this, all criticism to the contrary. In order to make the life of the little saint more interesting, there have been many attempts to prove that the conventional and snobbish Mother Prioress persecuted her, and that other stupid nuns followed her example. One tiny tale of a wash day in the convent, when a neighboring nun kept splashing dirty water in her face, is cited as a deliberate torment on the part of a brutal and clumsy sister. Although, as we shall see,

Therese was treated with greater severity than the ordinary
novice, she was not terrorized; little things have been exag-
gerated beyond recognition.

The life was hard enough. Therese said that when her
dream of gaining admittance was at last realized, "peace
flooded my soul, a deep, sweet, inexpressible peace; an in-
ward peace which has been my lot these eight and a half
years. It has never left me, not even when trials were at their
height. Everything here delighted me, our little cell most of
all; it was as though I had been transported to my faraway
desert."

She kept saying to herself that at last she was where she
wanted to be. "I am here forever now." It had been so hard
those last months; there had been the long period of waiting
and then the last days of farewell to the family, the last Holy
Communion together, the last breakfast in that much-loved
dining room, the parting with father and uncle and aunt,
cousins and sisters. They went with her to Carmel and after
Mass said good-by to her at the door. She felt at that moment
as though her heart would burst and that she would die. It
was a truly terrible moment, a fearful moment, but she was
always sure of just what she wanted. Her will was set on God.
God alone!

"Illusions!" She was to write eight years later. "Thanks to
God's mercy I had none at all; the religious life was just what
I had expected."

Because she was so young, only fifteen, the Prioress and
the Novice Mistress were afraid of seeming to indulge her and
so their reaction was extreme. She was given a more rigorous
testing than the others.

It must be remembered, too, that she had no gift for housework. Marie and then Celine had run the home; Therese was
clumsy, even untidy about such things. She had been the pet
of the family, the Benjamin, the last-born, the baby whose
entrancing ways attracted everyone. She was not only pretty,
she was good, ardent, loving. She had been her father's con-

stant companion, for there had been other girls to clean, sew, dust, keep house, and always, of course, the servants to bear the brunt of things. Now in the convent when Therese was set to dusting, her job was less than thorough, even though she did her best. The nuns saw dust everywhere, and once when a cobweb was discovered in a hall which she had been directed to tidy, the Prioress said harshly in front of everyone, "The cloisters are obviously swept by a fifteen-year-old; it is a disgrace! Go and sweep that cobweb away and in the future be more careful!"

Now and then she had to spend as much as an hour with Mother Marie de Gonzague for spiritual direction, and most of this time was given to a scolding. "And the worst of it was I did not know how to correct my faults; my slowness, for example, or my lack of generosity in carrying out my duties."

The Novice Mistress gave her a job of weeding the garden, probably because she had a young back and stoop labor was hard on the older nuns. Each day she ran into the Prioress on her way out and was rebuked again. "Really this child does nothing at all. There must be something wrong with a novice who has to be sent out for a walk every day."

But Therese had the wit to see that these pinpricks, indeed they might be called dagger thrusts, were of the stuff suffering is made of, and she accepted them with joy. One needs to have gone through these small martyrdoms to understand them. In the home a nagging relative, a husband or wife can be a source of misery. But Therese accepted it all as something of which she was in need. She knew she had "to die in order to live" and that every wound meant a killing of the ego. She was aiming for that perfection in which she could say with St. Paul, "It is now no longer I that live, but Christ lives in me." If she was going to work to save priests, through whose hands we receive the sacraments, the Bread of life, then this was the beginning of the accomplishment of this work.

For five years she followed this course, she said. She found it impossible to speak to her superiors of her method of dealing with problems, and the one priest whom she considered her spiritual director, Father Pichon, had been sent to Canada. Possibly she found it hard to speak because her "little way," as she termed it later, was not clearly formulated in her own mind. She had come to Carmel to be hidden, despised, following in the footsteps of her Master. She, too, had to be dumb as a sheep, not opening her mouth, until she tried to express these ideas in letters and in the chapters which she was bidden to write by her sisters later on. For one with great desires, great ambitions, a strong will, and a thirst for martyrdom in order to prove her love for God as well as to save souls, it was no doubt an act of humility to recount the little incidents, the little sufferings of her daily life which seem of so little account when put down on paper.

One of the first trials Therese had to suffer was to suppress another love of her heart toward creatures. Love of family she accepted, even advocated in her letters and writings. But when in the past her love had gone out to schoolmates, to her schoolmistresses, she had been rebuffed, almost as though she were unlovable; later she said that God had done great things for her in removing temptations from her, removing obstacles from her path that might have led her to fall into great sin.

And now the temptation recurs, the temptation to love too much her Mother Prioress. Just before her clothing—her espousals, as the nuns called them—when she had been in the convent nine months, she writes at the beginning of her retreat to her sister Pauline. This permission had been granted her perhaps because the Mother Prioress saw how hard it was for Therese to talk to her Superior.

She was looking forward to the day of her clothing because she would once again be permitted to see her father and her sister outside the grille, and because, perhaps, she felt that Jesus, her Spouse, would deliver her from her temptations to love creatures.

At the beginning of entering on her retreat many incidents came up to test her patience. She confessed to being in trouble with one of the Sisters and on the verge of tears. "Jesus riddles me with pinpricks," she complains. Recognizing her nothingness she had referred to herself as a little ball which the child Jesus played with or tossed aside. "The poor *little ball* can take no more; all over it are tiny holes which cause it more suffering than if it had but one great gash. Nothing from Jesus. Dryness! . . . Sleep! . . . But at least there is silence! Silence does good to the soul. But creatures! creatures! . . ."

She said she shuddered at the thought of them. She had to keep reminding herself that it was Jesus who pierced her with these small wounds and then she could feel suffering to be sweet. "Suffering is only sweetness, His hand is *so sweet!* . . . But creatures! . . . Those who surround me are good, of course, but there is a touch of something in them that repels me! I can't explain it to you. All the same I am VERY *happy,* happy at suffering what Jesus wants me to suffer. If He does not Himself pierce His *little ball,* it is He who guides the hand that pierces it."

She goes on to write that He sleeps, that He puts Himself to no trouble about her. "He shows me that I am not a stranger by treating me like this. I assure you He simply doesn't bother to make conversation with me."

Her desire to love was boundless. She wished to be indifferent to all the things of this world. What mattered all created beauties?

"Possessing them I should be utterly unhappy, my heart would be so empty. It's incredible how big a thing my heart seems when I consider the world's treasures . . . since all of them massed together would not content it . . . but how small a thing it seems when I consider Jesus! . . . I want to love Him so! . . . To love Him more than He has ever been loved! —My sole desire is to do the will of Jesus always."

When she expressed herself in this way to one of the priests who came to give the annual retreat to the Sisters, he rebuked

her for presumption and told her just to attend to her duties,
avoid her usual faults, and not try to be so ambitious. She
was no stranger to affronts. Another pinprick, she would
call it.

Looking forward to her clothing, when, dressed as a bride
in white satin and a magnificent and priceless veil of Alençon
lace such as her mother had spent her life in making, she
would be presented by her father to her Lord, she found herself in a state of great dryness. When the date of her clothing
was postponed, she writes:

> I suppose he found that the 9th [the day set for her
> clothing] delighted [me] too much. He wants [my soul] to
> have nothing to delight in. . . . And I know why, because
> He alone is delight in the full force of the word, and He
> wants to show His *little ball* that it would be a mistake to
> look elsewhere for a shadow of beauty which it might take
> for Beauty itself. He who will soon be my Spouse is so
> good to me, so divinely lovable in His determination not
> to let me attach myself to ANY created thing! He knows of
> course that if He let me have the bare *shadow* of HAPPI-
> NESS I should cling to it with all the energy, all the strength
> of my heart: this shadow He refuses me! . . . He would
> rather leave me in darkness than give me a false light that
> would not be *Himself*.
>
> Since I can find no created thing to content me, I will
> give all to Jesus, I will *not* to give to a creature even an
> *atom* of my love, may Jesus grant me always to realize
> that He alone is perfect happiness, even when He seems
> to be absent! . . .
>
> Today more than yesterday, if that be possible, I have
> been without any consolation. I thank Jesus, since He sees
> that that is good for my soul; perhaps if He gave me con-
> solations, I should rest in their sweetness, but He wants
> all to be for Him! Good! Then all *shall* be for Him, all!
> Even when I feel nothing that can be offered to Him, I
> shall (as tonight) give Him that nothing! . . .
>
> If Jesus does not give me consolation, He gives me a
> peace so great that it does me more good!

There is a footnote on page 81 of the *Collected Letters of St. Therese of Lisieux,* approved by Carmel and annotated by Abbé Combes, which says:

"As the starting point of this aspiration must be seen Therese's desire to live in perfect detachment with regard to the Prioress, Mother Marie de Gonzague. Later she confided to her the struggles this had caused her to undergo."

Therese's own words to Mother Marie de Gonzague, in a chapter of her autobiography addressed to her, are: "I remember that when I was a postulant I had often such violent temptations to seek my own satisfaction and find some drops of joy, that I was obliged to hurry past your cell and cling tight to the banisters to keep from retracing my steps. There came into my mind any number of permissions to ask, a thousand pretexts to give way to my nature and let it have what it craved. How happy I am now that I denied myself at the very beginning of my religious life!"

In a letter to her sister, begging her to pray for strength and courage for her, she complains that her heart had a burning thirst for happiness, but she realized, "that no creature can slake its thirst. It is exactly the reverse; the deeper it drinks at that enchanted spring, the more burning its thirst becomes."

The enchanted spring, Abbé Combes remarks, "is love for creatures, and the allusion is to her filial affection for Mother Marie de Gonzague."

Therese recognized that a desire to grow in the love of God has various ways of showing itself. On the one hand there may be irritation with others around us, a tendency to see only their faults, their unattractive ways, so that all natural love is pruned in order that a supernatural love may grow; on the other hand, the love of God may burst out in too vital a surge towards creatures, towards some one creature, and this delight must be stifled, must be understood and put down. She saw this in herself when she was fifteen years old, during that first year in Carmel. Three years later, she was able to help another novice quench this dangerous flame.

"She was eight years older than I," Therese tells, in the chapters which she addresses to the Mother Prioress toward the middle of her book. "But in spite of this we became intimate friends, and were allowed to talk together about spiritual matters to develop an affection which showed signs of helping us in the practice of virtue."

I was charmed by her innocence. She was so frank and open, yet her affection for you astonished me, for it was so different from mine, and her conduct seemed regrettable to me in many ways. But God has shown me already that in His mercy He never tires of waiting for some people, enlightening them only little by little, so I was careful not to rush things. Reflecting one day that we were allowed to talk in order, as the Rule says, "to inflame each other with a greater love for our Spouse," I realized sadly that the desired end was not being attained. It was clear that I should have to speak out or else really put an end to conversations which savored too much of the world. I implored our Lord to help me to speak gently but convincingly or rather, to speak through me, Himself. . . .

When we met for our next talk, the poor Sister saw at once from my manner that things were not the same as before. She blushed as she sat down beside me. I put my arms around her, and gently spoke my mind telling her what true love really is, proving that her natural affection for you was only a form of self-love, and making known the sacrifices I myself had to make at the beginning of my spiritual life in this very matter. Soon her tears were mingling with mine. She humbly admitted that I was right and she was wrong, promised to begin a new life, and asked me as a favor always to point out her faults.

From then on, our affection for one another became entirely spiritual, and the words of the Holy Spirit were fulfilled in us: "a brother that is helped by his brother is like a strong city."

You know very well, Mother, that I had no intention of turning her away from you, only of making it clear that true love feeds on sacrifice, and becomes more true and strong the more our natural satisfaction is denied.

And it is here that she confesses how she had had to do violence to herself in order to learn how to love. "I am only too glad now that I denied myself from the beginning of my spiritual life, for I enjoy already the reward promised to those who fight with courage. I no longer feel that I must deny my heart all consolation, for it is fixed on God. . . . It has loved Him alone, and this has gradually so developed it, that it is able to love those whom He loves with a tenderness incomparably deeper than any selfish, barren affection."

One of the reasons for stressing this struggle to attain to true love is St. Therese's statement that her mission was to make Love loved and to show that she was not dealing in abstractions. She never wrote anything that she had not experienced. She knew all aspects of love: love of mother, of father, and of family. Her love for her father enabled her to grow in her love for God her Father, an aspect of the Godhead that has been too much neglected. God the Father! She could say with Peguy that she knew what God the Father meant. His Son told the parable of the Prodigal Son and told how the father treated that son, welcoming the sinner with fatted calf, fine garment, and a ring for the hand which had turned so often to evil.

The first part of Therese's life was spent in illustrating to the world the tender love of a child for its father, the dependence, the trust of a creature for the Creator.

In the convent of Carmel she became the Spouse of Christ, and she did not hesitate to say that "He had kissed her with the kiss of His mouth" and to apply the glowing and sensuous words of the Canticle of Canticles to her relationship with Him. What did she know of men, this sheltered and cloistered girl, loved only by family and Sisters in religion? She had been an observant child, and had heard many things she was not meant to hear, on visits away from home, on holidays at Trouville and Deauville, on those days when she went to the home of a friend of the family to be tutored and on their pilgrimage to Rome. She heard many things, among them the terrible trial of Pranzini. She had observed men, and priests who were more men than priests. Therese knew the raptures of her cousin Jeanne in her engagement to a young doctor, and her later anxiety and grief at not having children. She knew the dangers that beset priests and nuns, too.

At that very time there was a famous Carmelite priest who had become an apostate and later had married. He went through France preaching and at the time of Therese's death he was still active. He died in 1912 at the age of eighty-five, assisted at the end by a schismatic Armenian priest and three Protestant pastors, but Therese was convinced that he would be saved, and later a Benedictine and a Jesuit wrote to the Carmel at Lisieux that they were convinced through supernatural means that at the end he had been saved by the intercession of Therese.

Sometimes it seems to me that nuns know more of sin in man than of the Christ in him, but it was not so with Therese. She knew the dangers of the world and she knew what was in man, but always her faith in her supernatural weapons was so great that she saw him as saved. Hers was not the vision of "sinners falling into hell like snow flakes," but of men at death seizing hold of a crucified Christ and embracing Him. Love was the measure by which she wished to be judged, and she sang of a merciful Father, of a Father who loved His children to folly. But she knew, too, that to love is to suffer, and just as a mother brings forth her children with anguish, she offered herself to the suffering that would result from her desire for souls. Who can doubt that God made "her, the barren woman, to dwell in her house, the joyful mother of children."

Yes, she knew men and the attraction towards men, why else the funny little incident recorded, when Celine and Leonie were going to balls with the Guerins, when she prayed that Celine would not be able to dance with a certain partner and lo! when they went out on the floor, they were held fast by some power other than themselves and could only walk, much to their great embarrassment.

She knew the longing for the love of companionship both at school and in those first months in Carmel, a longing for love which grew to such an extent that she recognized in this love "an enchanted spring," so that if she had partaken of it, she would have lived under enchantment instead of the reality she prayed always to face.

And beyond the immediate danger she recognized in these temptations the "delectation in temptation," and was rigid in turning from it. And so, knowing love in all its aspects and giving up love, she found love and lived in love.

But there was still greater intensity of suffering before her that first year of her life in Carmel.

The mental collapse of an adored father is so great a blow that one has to rally all one's forces to accept it in the light of faith. "In this great way," one might say, "I can show that I do 'believe that my Redeemer liveth and that in my flesh I shall see my God,' that Christ has triumphed over death, and that life here is but a moment compared to eternity. I do believe. I believe in God's love. Though He shall slay me yet shall I believe." The mind clings to these great truths at the time of immense sorrow, and a sense of the communion of saints lends strength to the weakest. One can be carried on even through long-enduring sorrow.

It was not long after Therese entered Carmel that her father had a second stroke. The first one had occurred before the pilgrimage, the second collapse came afterward. In February, the following year, after the "clothing" of Therese in the garb of a novice, he lost his mind completely. It was then that he had to be put into a mental hospital, Bon Sauveur, at Caen. This institution was like a town of 1,700 inhabitants, being made up of the religious community which served it, a boarding school, day school, school for the deaf and dumb, and an institution for mental cases.

Therese long before had had a prophetic vision of what was to occur to her father years later. When she was seven years old, she wrote, she "was alone at a window looking onto the large garden, my mind full of cheerful thoughts, when I saw before me, in front of the washhouse, a man dressed exactly like Papa, of the same height and appearance . . . for I did not see his face as his head was covered with a thick veil. He advanced slowly with measured step, along my little garden; at that instant a feeling of supernatural fear seized me, and I called out loudly in a trembling voice: 'Papa, Papa!' The mysterious person seemed not to hear, he continued his walk without even turning and went towards a clump of firs that grew in the middle of the garden. I expected to see him reappear at the other side of the big trees, but the prophetic vision had vanished."

Marie and Pauline heard her cries of terror and came running to her, and though they went into the garden and searched they found no one. They found it hard to reassure their little sister. After the father did indeed lose his memory and began suffering from amnesia, they remembered this vision. When these attacks began to come on him, he was ashamed, and used to cover his head with his arm, veiling his face as he had in the vision. "It was the time of his humiliation," the girls said.

It was as though he had given himself up to this trial. When he had given three daughters to the convent, and Leonie was also away, and he knew that later Celine would go, he had felt such a sense of joy and accomplishment, such a sense of honor that he had been enabled to return to God the gifts he had received, that he had a feeling of overwhelming rapture. Joy compelled him to offer himself still further to God. God had given him too much happiness, he said, and how was he to achieve heaven in this way, with so few trials, so few sorrows? Living in eternity as he did, the loss of his wife and the little ones born to them over the years meant only treasures in heaven. He felt afflicted by his wealth and offered himself to God.

Therese tells this in her autobiography. "Such a faithful servant deserved a fitting reward for his virtue, and you will remember, Mother, the reward he himself asked of God that day at visiting time when he said to us: 'I have just returned from Alençon. In the Church of Notre Dame, I received such great graces and consolations that I prayed: "It is too much, my God. I am too happy. This is not the way to Heaven; I want to suffer something for you, and I offer myself as a ..." ' the word victim died on his lips. He dared not say it in front of us, but we understood!"

Yet even while he was making such an offering he was making plans. He told Celine, "I am attached to life; it is not for myself but for my children. I want to buy Les Buissonnets. I shall arrange things for the best. I want to please you in everything."

He wanted security for his children, he wanted to do his duty as a father, yet he also wanted poverty. Therese recalls the jokes they had together at home, in a letter to her father the year after she entered the convent, thanking him for some gifts he sent, telling him that he will ruin himself. "But I shall surprise you by saying that I don't worry very much. After all you have so many resources, that you will never be short . . . even famine would not alarm you. Do you remember what you used to say? 'We shall eat this or that in the *famine*' or again, 'we'll do that when we are *ruined*.' "

He would not have anything to do with dealings on the stock market, but he did manage what property he had, investing capital in various undertakings that were useful as well as "safe." "I feel that I could easily become very interested in the skillful management of my fortune, but the slope is slippery," he once told Celine.

Soon he began to have compulsions to run away and on one occasion he disappeared for four days and was found later at Le Havre. He wanted to give his money away and was prevented by his brother-in-law Isidore, who had been appointed as joint guardian by Zelie before her death.

He had his lucid moments and well knew what fate had overtaken him when he entered Bon Sauveur. He had said of another condemned to such a confinement, "It is the hardest trial a man can undergo." To a Sister he said, "It is to humble my pride," and to the doctor, "I have never suffered a humiliation and I needed one. I am used to commanding and now I must obey."

For three years Louis Martin was confined there and for as long as they could obtain visiting privileges Celine and Leonie took rooms in an orphanage nearby to be with him, though their uncle wanted them to stay with his family.

The lease on Les Buissonnets had expired and it was as though the girls were homeless. Then another stroke made their father no longer capable of walking and so not capable of running away! This meant that he could be removed from the hospital and Isidore Guerin, the good brother-in-law, made arrangements for him in his own home. It was even possible to bring him once more, in a wheel chair, to the Carmel parlor so that he could see his other three daughters again. The meeting was so afflicting to him that all he could do was to point to the sky, as though to say that it was only in heaven that they would be able to speak to each other again.

This long illness, this tragic grief which only those can realize who have suffered it themselves, is treated by Therese in an extraordinary way: "My Father's three years of martyrdom seem to me the most desirable and fruitful years we have ever had, and I would not exchange them for the most sublime ecstasies."

Those same three years were also her first three years of co-suffering with Christ in Carmel.

XV

A Life of Work

ONE OF THE FOUNDRESSES of the Carmel at Lisieux was Mother Genevieve of St. Teresa, and she was the only one of the original group who was still alive when Therese entered the convent. By then she was a very old woman who kept to her bed in the infirmary. St. Therese evidently saw a good deal of her, as one would in a small community, and she felt that she had had the privilege of living for several years with a saint. "There were many occasions," she wrote, "when she gave me great consolation. One Sunday, for example, I went to see her in the infirmary and found two of the older Sisters with her. I was discreetly beating a retreat when she called me back, saying, as if in some way inspired: 'Wait, my child, I have something to say to you. You are always asking for a spiritual bouquet; very well, today I give you this one. Serve God in peace, and joy, and remember, our God is the God of peace.' "

It had been one of those days, Therese said, when she had been on the brink of despondency because of severe trials, but these words chased the shadows away and left her happy again. On the following Sunday she asked Mother Genevieve whether she had received any special revelation about the state of her soul on the previous week, but the aged nun insisted that she had known nothing at all of the state Therese was in, that she received no revelations. "This only increased my respect for her, for I saw to what an extent Jesus was

140

living in her soul, guiding her always. This seems to me the truest kind of holiness and the best; it is the kind of holiness I want because it is free from illusions."

Always she was praying that she would see things as they were, that she would live in reality, not in dreams.

Certainly she had little time to dream. There must have been a number of old nuns not capable of much work in a convent so long established, and that meant that the younger ones had a great deal of work to do. If there was a missionary spirit, as there seemed to be at Lisieux—nuns being sent out to other places to start new Carmels, a steady and organic growth—then one might say that there were not too many nuns to do the work of the cloister. There was the washing, the rinsing of which was generally done in cold water, a miserable job in the cold Norman winters, and of course there was never any hand-lotion for chapped red hands, cracked and swollen with chilblains. There was ironing, an interminable job what with the altar linens, the nuns' clothing, and everything to be done as perfectly as possible. There was the daily cleaning, the setting of tables and work in the kitchen, the work of the portress who answered the door and the turnstile, the work in the sacristy, the work in the garden. In addition to the baking and cooking and housework and washing, the nuns usually did something to earn money, such as embroidery, the painting of holy cards, and so on—the more delicate work being given to those considered the most talented.

One of the most important tasks in a convent where there are old nuns is the care of the sick, and often more than just an infirmarian is needed to do the work.

On Therese's nineteenth birthday, old Mother Genevieve died. She had been dying for some time, and on one occasion St. Therese had said to her, "You won't go to purgatory, Mother," and the old nun answered gently, "I hope not."

Considering the daily faults we all fall into, the tendencies of our human nature to evil, the failure in charity of thought if not of word and deed, considering, too, the well-known fact that temptations usually assault most strongly those who turn from the world and give themselves to God (witness St. Anthony), it is understandable that most Catholics feel that purgatory is essential to cleanse us from the stains of this life.

Cardinal Newman in his *Dream of Gerontius* speaks of the soul confronted by Divinity, flinging itself into purgatory most eagerly to make itself fit for the Beatific Vision. And Catherine of Genoa in her *Treatise on Purgatory* speaks of it as a place next in joy to heaven itself. The confidence in the last sacrament which the Little Flower always expressed, was not common in that day. She had no visions of hell as the Spanish Saint Teresa had. The French Therese's song was always of God the Father, and His mercy, God the Spouse and His love. She recognized His justice, and she had Masses offered for "her first child," Pranzini, but for Mother Genevieve she foresaw only the Beatific Vision.

Therese was present when the Mother Foundress died. She had been kneeling at the foot of the bed during her two-hour watch and feeling very guilty at the drowsiness that was overtaking her. Then at the very moment that Mother Genevieve died, the "state of soul" of the young sister was completely changed. "In the twinkling of an eye I was filled with joy, a joy I cannot describe. It was as if the saintly soul of our Foundress had at that moment given me a share in the happiness she enjoyed already, for I am sure she went straight to heaven."

About a month after this death, the first which Therese had ever witnessed, an influenza epidemic broke out in the convent. It occurred during the last two months of 1891 and every nun in the convent caught the dread disease. However, Therese and two others had light attacks and were able to keep going, though they were greatly overburdened. "The worst cases were looked after by others who could scarcely drag themselves about." Death reigned everywhere, and no sooner had a Sister breathed her last than she had to be left, "to go on and work with the living."

Therese speaks about the death of a former Prioress, the

Infirmarian, and two others. How many were there who were able to attend Mass in the morning? She does not speak of her own sisters, Pauline and Marie. All the women in the convent were her sisters now and she loved them all.

One morning as she wakened she had the presentiment that another very ill Sister, Magdalene, was no longer alive. Evidently the sick were left in their cells, perhaps the infirmary was not big enough to contain them all. At that early hour no one was stirring and the corridors were icy cold. Therese entered the cell of Sister Magdalene and found her lying fully dressed on her mattress. She was dead. It was Therese's job to run to the sacristy for a blessed candle to disperse the gloom of the cell, and to bring the crown of roses to place above the poor gaunt face of the deceased sister.

No letters, no communications with her sisters are left to us from this time; there are two blank months when, from dawn to dark, duties pressed upon those who were still up and about. How few their numbers now! How little cooking needed to be done! But how greatly increased was the washing, as in all sicknesses. Probably many a good housewife came often to bring cooked food that would save work for the well Sisters and tempt the appetites of the convalescent.

Therese's tender nursing of the ill during these months must have won the hearts of the other Sisters at Carmel. We know that the privilege of daily Communion was given her at this time, although it was still withheld from the others.

When the other Sisters were up and about again, and the work divided once more, Therese, for the first time was given a chance to play with paints and brush. Years before when the father had offered to pay for lessons for Pauline, who showed much talent, and had brought her vellum and ivory and paints from Paris, he ignored the desires of his youngest, thinking perhaps that anyone so clumsy, as she said she was at household tasks, could not be proficient at finer work. At any rate he never offered her lessons, and she made it a matter of sacrifice not to ask. It was a matter of practice on the part of the child to go out of her way to find *good* things to give up, as an offering to God, and not only imperfections.

So added to her usual duties was the job of painting pictures, and even murals on a chapel wall. She had much joy in her artistic activities.

There was work during those years, including the usual studies undertaken by the novices. One of the studies must have been Latin, for that is the language in which the Sisters chanted the Office, which is made up of the Psalms and readings from the Fathers of the Church. Yet there was still time for spiritual reading. Between the ages of sixteen and eighteen, Therese wrote, she read no one but St. John of the Cross, and over and over again in her autobiography she quotes from him, especially from his poetry. Perhaps it was his poetry that led her to write poetry, and this talent once discovered meant that she was called upon, like a court poet, to produce verses for feast days, name days, anniversaries— truly a task. It was to be done in her spare time, so doubtless she was forced to concentrate on the task, much as a newspaper reporter has to work over an assignment, and commit her painfully composed verses to memory until she had some time in the evening after Compline, when the prayer of the day was completed, to put the words down on paper.

So much time has been spent in apologizing for the flowery setting of the thoughts of Therese, that not much attention has been given to her poetry, which is simple and fresh and filled with love and longing for God.

According to the Benedictine Rule, the *Opus Dei*—the work of God which must come before all other work—is that of offering up the Holy Sacrifice of the Mass and reciting the Divine Office.

So the prime work of the Carmelite is to acquire a love for and a knowledge of God as well as to praise Him. This Rule obliges her to recite the Breviary—an obligation that is also assumed by priests. The Carmelite also fits reading and meditation into her schedule. Altogether seven hours may be given to prayer each day, in addition to the manual labor of the cloister. Unlike the secular, or diocesan, clergy, the monk and the nun are obliged to chant the Office, and this in itself is a physical work, taking the strength and the breath of the body. Anyone who has had long hours of reading to an invalid will know that such an employment of the voice can also be work.

Observance of penance and mortification also is a work. The Rule calls for a fast according to the calendar of the Church, from September 14 until Easter, which means bread and a hot drink as a morning refreshment after hours in the chapel, one meal a day, and a collation in the evening, which may mean only a drink and bread and cheese. No flesh meat is allowed, but fish and fowl are permitted at the main meal, aside from days of stricter fast. No wonder Louis Martin's gifts of fresh-caught fish were so welcome.

Therese experienced these and other privations. Her habit was of coarse serge, her stockings of rough muslin, and on her feet she wore rope sandals. Her bed was made of three planks, covered by a thin pad and one woolen blanket. There was scarcity of food, inadequate bedding, no heat in the convent except for one small stove in one room. Prayer and penance! These are indeed spiritual works, spiritual weapons to save souls, penance for luxury when the destitute suffer, a work to increase the sum total of love and peace in the world.

Six or seven hours of prayer, a life of hard work in silence the rest of the time, two brief periods of recreation when there was permission to talk, sew, paint, or take up the "busy work" all women delight in. In addition to the works of the community, whether it was laundry, kitchen, dining room, sacristy, much of the work was done alone. When it came to the sewing, the fine embroidery done by the community, the tradition was to work in one's cell.

Much of the convent's physical work was carried on under very difficult circumstances. The Sisters, of course, had none of the machinery that makes today's household tasks relatively easy. There is a picture showing Celine and Therese bending over the stone washtubs, laughing together. But it was no laughing matter to stand outdoors during winter, rinsing the linen in cold water. Therese always tried to take the most difficult tasks, feeling that it was the part of charity to do so since she would be saving another Sister the hard labor. It was the same with the hot, steamy laundry in summer. When there was a choice of work, she took the hardest, not only as a penance but as an act of loving kindness, a practice in love. One could not love God without loving His household.

And whatever she did, she did with the utmost cheerfulness, always with a gentle smile, with briskness and alacrity. "She ran in the way of His commandments since He enlarged her heart," as the Psalmist wrote. When she had other work and could not be present at recreation, the Sisters used to say that on those occasions there was little laughter. Therese was a mimic, could tell a story, always knew how to see the funny side of things in the little incidents that came up in convent life.

Her only reason for telling about the irritations encountered in her life with twenty others under obedience, was to show of what little things the practice of virtue is made up.

XVI

Spiritual Development

BY THE TIME she was twenty, Therese had gone through many intense experiences, losing father and mother, feeling an orphan but emphasizing for that reason her dependence on God as a Father. Over and over again through her writings "God appears to her understanding," writes Father Liagre, "and above all to her heart (for she lived much more by her heart than her understanding) as a Father, as her Father, as the most affectionate and tender of fathers; in a word as fatherly love, and that at its very highest perfection . . . 'The Father . . . of whom all paternity in heaven and earth is named.' It is the very essence of the Gospel teaching that God is our Father. . . . Therese is the living commentary on the Gospels, the most beautiful commentary because the most simple."

Her mother died when Therese was so young in order that, one might say, she would emphasize this father-love, this father-mother love, as Juliana of Norwich calls it. One can only go to the Father through Jesus, so she not only spoke of herself as Spouse of Christ, as all nuns are, but also as the playfellow, the plaything, even, of the Child Jesus. Her familiarity with God the Father, God the Son, and God the Holy Spirit might be called her recognition of the immanence of God, and this very familiarity which leads her to liken herself to a little plaything, a ball, a little grain of dust to be trampled underfoot, points to God's transcendence, to the infinite distance between God and creatures. On the one hand He is closer than the air we breathe, and on the other hand we are the grain of sand on the seashore, lost in the nothingness before the All Powerful.

Her life at home with her sisters, her training at school and at home, all was directed Godward. Even the holidays at Trouville, the pilgrimages, the little visits in the country served to remind her always of God. She examined the events of her life, her eating and drinking, her rising up and sitting down, her speech and her silence, in the light of the love of God. "Whether we eat or whether we drink, do all in the name of the Lord Jesus Christ." "That in all things God may be glorified." The slow peaceful current of her days carried her on, as the river in which her father fished, peaceful under the wide sky and broad meadows and orchards of Normandy. She lived by the river rather than by the sea with its immensity.

Her life in the convent with its hemmed-in days, its small duties, always the same twenty nuns, the same tasks, the same routine of the day, was yet all lit up by the glory of the Office. Its first words are: "Open O Lord my mouth, unto praise of Thy Holy Name. Cleanse also my heart from all vain, perverse and distracting thoughts. Enlighten my mind, inflame my heart, that I may recite this office worthily, attentively and devoutly and deserve to be heard in the presence of Thy Divine Majesty, through Christ, our Lord, Amen."

Matins, Lauds, Prime, Terce, Sext, None, Vespers and Compline. Seven times daily the praise of God rose to the sky. And at the end of the day, by ten o'clock (the rising was at five-thirty), the closing prayer:

"May praise, power, honor and glory be given by every creature throughout all eternity to the most holy and undivided Trinity, the humanity of our Lord Jesus Christ, the chaste motherhood of Mary, the ever glorious and blessed Virgin, and to the company of all the saints; and may we obtain the remission of all our sins through all eternity.

"Blessed is the womb of the Virgin Mary, that bore the

Son of the Eternal Father. And blessed are the breasts that gave sustenance to Christ the Lord. Amen."

Therese had visitors, not only from her own family, with whom she was permitted to draw aside the curtain of the grille, but from women of the world who were acquainted with her family and who often brought her their problems. She wrote to Celine while her sister was still at home caring for their father:

"How fortunate we are to have been chosen by the Spouse of Virgins! N— has confided to us intimate secrets which she tells to no one. We must certainly pray for her, for she is under grave temptation . . . She says that no book does her any good." And then Therese asks that Celine bring this woman a book which had brought Therese great comfort, if she could get it to her without her husband, or even the aunts and relatives of the Martin girls, knowing anything about it. The book she was still recommending after four years in the convent, and after reading St. John of the Cross, learning the *Imitation of Christ* by heart, is *The End of Time and Mysteries of the Future Life* by Abbé C. Arminjon, a book long out of print. One would like to see this book which was such a favorite with Therese.

Then Louis Martin was brought home from the mental hospital and spent the summer at La Musse, a beautiful country home with forty acres of grounds, which had been inherited at that time by Isidore and his wife from a member of the wife's family. Even when Mr. Martin and his two daughters, Leonie and Celine, took another house in Lisieux, there were times when Celine went away for short visits to the country leaving Leonie to take care of the father. The girls corresponded through these years, Celine, Leonie, Marie and Jeanne (the cousins), the four outside, writing to the three in Carmel. Three of the four were to enter religion later. Jeanne married a Dr. Neele. The occasion of her marriage made Therese realize still more how much she must try to please her own Spouse, and the wonderful dignity that was hers in the nuptials which made her "one flesh," divinity itself, through this Bridegroom.

During the influenza epidemic she had proven to the community and to Father Delatroette, who had so opposed her entry into Carmel, the sturdiness of her nature, her faithfulness to detail, her dependability, her unfailing sweetness.

When she had entered, tall, slender, composed, she had surprised them with all this dignity. They had expected a child of fifteen, but her height, her composure, her great self-control astonished them. She had a maturity which they did not expect. Her own recognition of her youth and inexperience had made her keep much to the background, cling to silence, hide from notice, those first years. It is part of the rule of Carmel never to defend oneself from false accusations, never to answer charges made against one, but to kiss the ground in humility and accept whatever accusations of neglect or carelessness are made against one, such as the breaking of a vase, a failure to respond to a call for help from another, and so on. But when all the Sisters were laid low and had to be nursed by the two who had not been stricken, Therese had perforce to assume an authority, an initiative which showed her worth.

It was not long after this that Mother Marie de Gonzague finished her term of office and Mother Agnes of Jesus (Pauline) was elected Prioress.

This gave rise to a delicate situation—how to deal with a woman of such suspicious and prideful disposition as the former Prioress. A letter to the new Prioress, refers to a "veil cast over the day" and a footnote in the *Letters* says "Certain circumstances had cast a gloom over her election." It might have been family circumstances, but then again the temperament of Mother Marie de Gonzague made the election so difficult a one that Therese wrote her a letter of consolation.

The situation was handled by the Martin sisters with consummate delicacy. Mother Marie de Gonzague was made Novice Mistress, and since she was obviously unfit by her moody temperament for this job, her assistant was Therese!

Pauline was elected in February, 1893, and in the summer Mr. Martin died. Six weeks later, Celine entered Carmel. For a few weeks there had been opposition on the part of one Sister but that was soon withdrawn. With the entrance of Marie Guerin, Therese had five postulants to instruct, two of them relatives.

After Jeanne's marriage, when she had moved to Caen, another Norman town, she wrote to Therese of her illnesses and the great desire of the Neele's to have a baby. Therese answered and advised them to pray to St. Anne, the patroness of grandmothers. In the same letter there is reference to chocolate, and to coffee-cream and pastries which Jeanne had sent for a feast day. The letters are full of gratitude for the gifts sent to the nuns from the relatives of the Martins. There were only twenty, so it was easy to send treats to them; even at that there was not room for self-indulgence. One remembers the stories of the convents in Spain at the time of Teresa of Avila. Many women took refuge in them because of family trouble, and unmarried and delicate daughters were put away. The convents grew so large that there was not sufficient food to feed all the nuns. The poverty and scarcity of food was one of the reasons for laxity, because the nuns were only too anxious to go to the parlors to entertain relatives and guests who brought something to eat.

There was never any suspicion of laxity in the convent at Lisieux. Therese talks frankly of little gifts of lobster, champagne, but she always made a point of seeing that any delicacies were divided among the others. The story was that she was so indifferent to what she ate that all the leftovers, the indigestible rejects from former meals, could be served up to her at the one main meal where a certain abundance of food could be set out.

If there was enough food at Lisieux there certainly was not enough heat, and Therese confessed at the end of her life that the thing she suffered from the most was the cold. She had been so cold that she thought she would have died of it.

It was in the spring of 1896, in April, that she received the first warning of the sickness that caused her death. She had been seven years in Carmel and had kept the rule as no other nun had kept it. Even as Novice Mistress she had been under the strict rule of Mother Marie de Gonzague (elected Prioress again after Pauline's term), who had suffered so little physically herself that she did not recognize the symptoms of exhaustion and pain in others. Even in those previous three years when Pauline was Prioress, Mother Marie had been Novice Mistress and Therese had had to work under her. Henri Gheon comments that it would not have done for Therese to have died under the regime of Pauline, who might have been accused not only of pampering her, but of exaggerating her sufferings in view of her later canonization.

Therese tells the story of the beginning of her illness, how on going to her cell one night in the bitter cold, and undressing in the dark, she suffered a hemorrhage from the lungs which soaked her handkerchief with blood. She did not even light her lamp but lay down on her hard pallet to take the few hours of sleep allowed Good Friday night. She says she was overwhelmed with joy at the thought that she was going to go soon to God. She did not lie awake since it was already midnight, but she woke with a sense of expectation, as though she had something good and exciting to look forward to, and going to the window, saw that her handkerchief was all stained with blood. She reported it, as it was her duty to do, to Mother Marie de Gonzague, and begged to be allowed to finish Lent with the same austerity as usual and the permission was given. There were long hours in the cold chapel, the only fire was in the recreation room, and they probably did not have that during Holy Week. Normandy winters are cold and damp, the penetrating cold of a New England as contrasted with the dry cold of a Minnesota. Anyone who has ever suffered the desolation of cold can realize what the Little Flower had to endure. On her insistence those last days of her life, the convent was heated after her death.

As Therese went right on working and following the practice of never letting anyone notice her fatigue, the pain she endured, not much attention was paid to her illness. With summer and better food her cough disappeared for a time. But to prevent a recurrence she had to go through the remedies prescribed at the time, blistering, cupping, cauterizing and so on. As was said of the woman with an issue of blood, she suffered much from doctors.

The first eight chapters of her autobiography came to be written in this way: While Mother Agnes of Jesus was in office she and Sister Marie of the Sacred Heart (Marie Martin) and Therese were talking together during recreation. Therese was asked to tell to the community some of the stories of her childhood. She had always been a good storyteller and it was that talent that had won friends for her at the Benedictine convent where she went to school. She was a mimic, she was vivacious and cheerful. The recreation was so enjoyable that Marie asked Pauline if she would not, by virtue of her authority as Superior, order her little sister to write an account of her childhood and education.

Time and time again St. Therese talked about her need to instruct others in her "little way." Not the least striking reference is one noted by Pauline at a time when Celine was hesitating as to whether to join Father Pichon, "the director of the Martin household," who was now in Canada and was starting some new work. Therese spoke of the readiness we should all have to do God's will, to suffer, to be parted from our nearest and dearest, and pointed out how often God only wanted this readiness, this acceptance, and then did not exact of us the sacrifice we were prepared to make.

Therese longed for Celine to be with her and told her older sister at the close of her life of this longing. "Often, during the summer, in the evening silence, sitting on the terrace I said to myself: 'Ah, if my Celine were here with me . . . but no, it would be too great a happiness . . .' and it seemed to me beyond possibility, but it was not by nature that I desired this happiness, it was for her soul, that she might walk in our way. . . . And when I saw her entered here, and not only entered but given over wholly to me for her instruction in all

things, when I saw that the good God went so far beyond my
desires, I realized what an immensity of love He had for me."

She knew with a certainty beyond doubt that she was
teaching the way of the early Christians, the way Jesus Himself spoke of when He said, "I am the Way, the Truth and
the Life."

And she did not hesitate to teach her oldest sister, Marie,
who asked her before her death to write a special chapter for
her in her *Story of a Soul.*

She knew with a certainty that is heaven itself, or a fore-
taste of heaven, that she had been taught the secret, the
"science of love." She died saying, "Love alone matters."
She died saying that she did not regret having given herself
up to love.

Her secret is generally called the Little Way, and is so
known by the Catholic world. She called it little because it
partakes of the simplicity of a child, a very little child, in its
attitude of abandonment, of acceptance.

We know of course that not all children, not even infants,
are so gifted. But generally speaking, the little child is dependent and trustful, ready to accept everything from the
hand of its parent, with no knowledge of prideful independ-
ence. Therese is content to be considered always the little
child, the little grain of sand, the creature who can give nothing to its Creator but the willing acceptance of this status,
taking from the hand of its Creator all that comes in daily life.

"Count any day lost in which one does not receive some
suffering, some insult, some lesson to put one in one's place,"
she seems to cry out with Father Lallemant, the Jesuit spiritual writer. "Know thyself," she cries out with St. Augustine,
"that you are nothing and that He is All. That if He let you
go for a minute you would utterly cease to be. That God
dwells in your soul, that the principle of natural and supernatural life are both from God, and he sustains you even in
your sin, that He collaborates even in sin, that He is dragged
down into sin in that He sustains our life, breathing into us
the breath of life."

She writes that she does not learn from books, because by the end of her short life she can no longer read St. John of the Cross, the writings of the saints or à Kempis. The words of the Bible are engraved in her heart. She can scarcely even pray, aside from the Office. She lives in dryness and utter aridity, having no comfort, her comfort being to have no comfort. "My joy," she writes, "consists in being deprived of all joy here on earth." She has asked for this early in life, that God would turn all things sweet into bitterness for her so that she will not be attracted to things of earth, or even to things of heaven, since it is her Beloved alone that she wants.

"I wish for no other knowledge," she cries, "and like the Spouse in the Canticle of Canticles, 'having given up all the substance of my house for love, I reckon it as nothing.' "

She knows that God has said, "to him that is little, mercy is promised. He will be carried at the breasts and upon the knees they shall caress you. As one whom the mother caresseth, so will I comfort you."

And if it is sometimes hard for us to understand what Therese means, she herself writes to her sister Marie, "I dare not try to understand all that my prayer means, O my God! I should fear to be crushed by the mere weight of its audacity. That I am thy child is my only excuse, for children do not grasp the full meaning of their words."

Knowing how important is this way of love in the world today, she closed her chapter to her sister with this prayer to God: "I beseech Thee to cast Thy glance upon a vast number of little souls: I entreat Thee to choose in this world a legion of little victims worthy of Thy love."

Father Henry Petitot, the Dominican, gives an interesting account of how the last of Therese's story came to be written. After Mother Marie de Gonzague had been reelected, and "Mother Agnes after her one term of three years had time on her hands again, as a simple nun" she took up the manuscript and went over it again and was much struck by its charm. Therese had never mentioned the manuscript again, once she had handed it to her sister on her feast day when she was

Prioress. (It is an indication of the silence and mortification she practiced that her older sisters did not even know of her illness until some time after her hemorrhages.)

Seeing Sister Therese of the Child Jesus so ill [Mother Pauline wrote], four months before her death, I went to Mother Prioress: "Mother," I said, "I cannot sleep until I have told you a secret. Whilst I was Prioress, Sister Therese wrote down some remembrances of her childhood under obedience and in order to give me pleasure. These I read over again the other day; they are very pretty, but you will not get much out of them to help you in writing her obituary notices, for there is very little about her life in religion. If you tell her to do so, she might write something more serious, and I am certain you would have something far better than what I have." Our Lord blessed my enterprise and the next morning our Mother bade Sister Therese of the Child Jesus to continue her story. I had already chosen an exercise book for her, but she thought it was too good, though it was quite an ordinary one, and she was afraid she might commit a fault against holy poverty by using it. She asked me whether she ought not at least to write between the lines so as to use less paper. I answered that she was too ill to tire herself by writing like that, and that she ought on the contrary to leave plenty of space between the lines and write very large.

It took Therese a month to write fifty pages. The last lines, written in pencil, because she was too weak to hold a pen, were these:

"It is not because I have been preserved from mortal sin that I lift up my heart to God in love and trust. I feel that even if I had on my conscience every crime one could commit, I should lose nothing of my confidence; my heart broken with sorrow, I would throw myself into the arms of my Saviour. I know that He loves the prodigal son, I have heard His words to St. Mary Magdalene, to the woman taken in adultery, and to the woman of Samaria. No one could frighten me, for I know what to think of his mercy and his love."

Although the chapters are not given any headings or divisions as she wrote them, when the work was edited her superiors did not hesitate to entitle the chapter that begins her account for Mother Marie de Gonzague, "The Dark Night of the Soul."

XVII

Night and Death

THERESE BEGINS the third part of her autobiography by telling the story of the hemorrhage she suffered on the eve of
Good Friday and speaks of her joy at the idea of death, her
approaching entrance into a new life.

Her joy, in fact, kept her from feeling any pain or fatigue,
and she was allowed to go on with all the exercises of Carmel
during that most holy day. That night when she went to bed,
she again suffered a hemorrhage. "My faith at this time was
so clear and so lively that the thought of Heaven was my
greatest delight; I could not believe it possible that there
should be wicked men without Faith and I was sure that those
who deny the existence of another world belie their convic-
tions. But during the Paschal days, that time so full of light,
Our Lord made me understand that there are really souls
bereft of faith and hope, which through the abuse of grace
have lost these precious gifts, the only source of pure and
lasting joy."

By this last sentence it is plain that she was not just thinking of those who have no faith, who have had no religious
instruction, no knowledge of the supernatural life, but of
those who by mortal sin, by not "corresponding to grace,"
as St. Paul has it, have fallen into the blackness of despair.

[God] allowed my own soul to be plunged in thickest
gloom, and the thought of Heaven, so sweet from my earli-

est years, to become for me a subject of torture. Nor did
the trial last merely for days or weeks; months have passed
in this agony and I still await relief. I wish I could explain
what I feel but it is beyond my power. One must have
passed through the tunnel to understand how black is the
darkness. Let me try, however, to illustrate what I mean.

I will suppose that I was born in a land of thick fog, that
I had never seen nature in her smiling moods or one single
ray of sunshine. From my childhood I had heard of these
things and knew that the country in which I dwelt was not
my real home, that there was another land to which I must
always aspire. This was no fable invented by an inhabitant
of the land of fogs. It was an unquestionable truth, for the
King of that sunlit country had come to dwell for three and
thirty years in the land of darkness, though alas! *"the
darkness did not comprehend that He was the light of the
world."*

But dear Jesus, Thy child believes firmly that Thou art
the Light Divine; she asks pardon for her unbelieving
brethren and is willing to eat the bread of sorrow as long
as Thou will it so. For love of Thee she will sit at the table
of bitterness where these poor sinners take their food and
will not rise from it till Thou givest the sign. But may she
not say in her own name and in the name of her guilty
brethren: *"O God be merciful to us sinners."* Send us away
justified. May all those on whom faith does not shine at
last see the light! My God, if that table which they profane
must be purified by one who loves Thee, I am willing to
remain there alone to eat the bread of tears until the day
when it shall please Thee to bring me to Thy kingdom of
light. I ask no other favor beyond that of never offending
Thee.

Not long ago I read a biography of St. Ignatius in which
the author said that when Ignatius was lying ill with his
wounds during his life as a soldier and had nothing else to
read he began with the life of Christ, and was so impressed
by the words of Jesus that he took to copying them down
laboriously, in red ink. When I copy down these written
words of Therese about the blackness of her night, I realize

them more clearly and see more clearly, too, her great love and great desire for *all* men. She prays for all men with that holy optimism of Charles Péguy in his great poem, "God Speaks," where he compares the folded hands of Jesus in the Our Father to the prow of a ship which ploughs on ahead through the waves, and in its wake draws all along after it. She too cries out for mercy for all, not just for her family, for France, for Christians, but for all.

I have already told you, Mother [she continues], that from my childhood, I had had the conviction that I should one day be released from this land of darkness. I believed it not only from what I had heard, but also because the deepest and most secret longings of my heart assured me that there was in store for me another and most beautiful country, an abiding dwelling place. I was like Christopher Columbus whose genius anticipated the New World. But of a sudden, the fog that surrounds me finds its way into my very soul, and so blinds me that I can no longer see there the lovely picture of my promised home . . . it has all faded away.

When my heart, weary of the enveloping darkness, tries to find some rest and strength in the thought of an everlasting life to come, my anguish only increases. It seems to me that the darkness itself, borrowing the voice of the unbeliever, cries mockingly: "you dream of a land of light and fragrance, you believe that the Creator of these wonders will be yours forever, you think to escape one day from the mists in which you now languish. Hope on! Hope on! Look forward to death! It will give you, not what you hope for, but a night darker still, the night of utter nothingness!"

This description of what I suffer, dear Mother, is as far removed from reality as the painter's rough outline from the model he copies, but to write more might be to blaspheme . . . even now I may have said too much. May God forgive me! He knows how I try to live by faith, even though it affords me no consolation. I have made more acts of faith during the past year than in all the rest of my life.

She says that she wants to offer this blackness for all those in the world today who do not believe, who "have lost the precious treasures of faith and hope and with them all joy that is pure and true." She says she has no sense of joy whatever, and yet she can still say, "Thou hast given me, O Lord, a delight in Thy doings." Since it is suffering of a most cruel kind that she is laboring under, a blackness of the mind and soul, she "wills" a delight in this suffering. If suffering is a part of love, suffering then will become her delight.

To the community she gave every appearance of serenity and peace, and yet "in peace is my bitterness most bitter" she quotes. On another occasion she says, "Let us suffer if needs be, with bitterness." She, the realist, well knew that suffering of body and soul is not lofty and exalted, but mean and cruel, a reflection of the blackness of hell. It was not suffering for itself that she embraced. It was a means to an end; the very means used by Jesus Himself.

In order to hide this suffering from others, she wrote poems about the joys of faith, hope and charity, and yet in the night of sense and soul that she was passing through, she felt none of these joys. She wanted her suffering to be hidden even from God, if that were possible, in order to atone for lack of faith in the world. She asked consolation from no one, not even from God. She had wanted martyrdom, and this heavy weight of despair is martyrdom.

When I sing of Heaven's happiness, of what it is to possess God forever, I feel no joy [she writes]. I simply sing *of what I want to believe*. Now and then, I must admit, a gleam of light shines through the dark night, to bring a moment's respite, but afterwards, its memory, instead of consoling me, only makes my night darker than ever.

Yet I realize as never before that the Lord is gentle and merciful; He did not send me this heavy cross until I could bear it. If He had sent it before, I am certain that it would have discouraged me, but now it merely takes away from me any natural satisfaction I might feel in longing for Heaven.

It seems to me at the moment that there is nothing to prevent my flying away, because I desire nothing at all now except to love until I die of love. I am free, I am not afraid of anything; not even of what I used to dread most of all . . . a long illness which would make me a burden to the community. . . . I am perfectly content to go on suffering in body and soul for years if it would please God.

To understand something of the physical sufferings of St. Therese it is necessary to remember the routine life led by these nuns even today in seven hundred Carmelite convents in the world. Here in the United States alone there are fifty-three Carmels, housing eight hundred nuns, located in twenty-nine of the states. Although the Carmelites sleep on two planks with a mattress of straw, between two rough woolen sheets, winter and summer, and without milk, eggs and cheese during Lent, the penance which is most severe is fatigue.

"There is never a moment, from 5:30 in the morning until eleven at night when she retires, when a nun can 'completely relax,' " a New York Carmelite has written. "Except during the summer months, when the rising time is an hour earlier, and there is a siesta of an hour at midday, a nun is never allowed to lie down on her bed. During all those hours in her cell, working, sewing, praying, reading, studying, she sits in an upright chair, and even all her movements are prescribed. She must stand, sit, walk, kneel, hold her hands, her head, her eyes, in a certain way, learning a complete control of the body as a discipline and a penance.

"Even in the chapel we must kneel without the support of a kneeling bench and hold our office books in a proper manner. Once when I was observed leaning against the wall, I was reminded that the Carmelite leans on nothing but God. Fighting back this constant feeling of fatigue is the most difficult of penances."

During this period of spiritual and physical suffering, Therese was able, she said, to go on with all the exercises of the religious life, even the hardest manual labor. She went on washing windows, washing clothes and the work was laborious indeed. Sometimes she could scarcely walk up the stairs she was so exhausted, but went from step to step, breathing heavily, scarcely able to lift one foot after the other. Sometimes it took her an hour to undress, the effort was so great.

She never complained, she went on with the work of the day in chapel and out of it, and said nothing. The rule calls for complete silence except during the two hours of recreation, one after the noonday meal, and the other after the evening collation. At these times she was merry, there was always a smile to disguise the deadly fatigue, and no mention was made of the fact that she was dying by inches.

There has been a great deal of talk and writing about the fact that the Carmel of Lisieux touched up the photographs which were taken of Therese four months before her death. She was always a round-faced, merry child and in the painting her sister Celine made of her, "a composite picture" it was called, there was an attempt made to "refine" her, to hollow the cheeks, to give a more ascetic look, a more nun-like contour. Even these pictures taken of Therese within a few months of her death, though showing her drawn and haggard, with black circles under the eyes, and an expression of pain about the mouth, show a broad face, not a thin, ascetic one. One could know nothing of the emaciation of the body.

Father Martindale, the British Jesuit, spoke out with indignation about this tampering with the pictures. In view of the gigantic role she was to play in the life of the Church, one can understand this wrath. Even her writing, her autobiography, her *Story of a Soul* was worked over, her strong expressions toned down, and it is only recently that we have had an authentic translation of her manuscript.

When her sisters reproached her at the end for not telling them of her sufferings, so that they could have cared for her and made her days and nights easier, she expressed herself as glad that they had not known; for if they had seen the neglect she suffered, their hearts would have broken, she said.

For Mother Gonzague was a hard woman and, not suffering any illnesses herself, was not lenient with those who were sick. For more than a year Therese continued her duties, slept in her cell at the end of a long cold corridor. In the winter months, after warming herself at the monastery's one fire, she hastened down the long cold corridors, out through the cloister and on to her cell. Every night she went to bed on her straw mattress chilled to the bone under her thin cover.

Before the end, she became skin and bones. Father Petitot said that she became so thin that her bones protruded through her skin. Tuberculosis of the intestines set in and gangrene, and when she was raised up in bed to get her breath, she gasped that it was as though she were sitting on spikes. Sometimes she could not breathe without crying out at each breath. Yet she kept on trying to work. She wanted to stay in her cell so that her coughing at night would not disturb the others. She was finally moved to the infirmary and when the summer came she was wheeled out to sit in the garden, and it was then that she tried to write those last chapters of her book.

As she sat writing in the garden, the novices (there were probably only three or four) used to run out to speak to her, and the nuns did not hesitate to interrupt her. When she was commended for her patience, she admitted how difficult it was, what a nerve-wracking strain, but added, "If I am trying to write about brotherly love, it would be a pity if I could not be practicing it."

Early in the month of July the manuscript was turned over to Mother Agnes, her sister, and from then on Therese became so ill that her sisters, attending her, wished that she could die and be out of her pain.

"You ought not to say that, Little Mother, because to suffer is exactly what pleases me in life," she answered.

Since May Pauline had been jotting down some things she said, and this notebook is now published under the name of *Novissima Verba*.

"She reminded me of the words of St. John of the Cross," Pauline wrote. " 'Break the web of this sweet encounter.' I have always applied those words to the death of love which I desire. Love will not wear out the web of my life, it will break it suddenly. With what desire and consolation I have repeated to myself from the commencement of my religious life these other words of St. John of the Cross: 'It is of the highest importance that the soul exercise itself much in love, so that its course may be quickly finished, and being but little delayed here below, it may quickly come to see God face to face!' "

On July 29, 1897, the nuns were afraid that she was going to die during the night and she spoke to them of her capacity for suffering. She had not realized she could endure so much. But—"I have never had much capacity for enjoyment; I have always noticed that; but I have a great capacity for suffering . . . My body has always inconvenienced me; I have never been at home in it . . . and even when quite a little child it caused me confusion."

The flies tormented her very much during that last hot summer. It must have been no little part of the suffering of Christ on the Cross, nailed and enduring the crawling of flies on His eyes, His wounds, His flesh. "They are my only enemies," Therese said when she was tormented by them. "God commanded us to forgive our enemies, and I am glad I have some occasion to do so. That is why I spare them."

She had a great sense of the importance of her mission but she said, "No, I do not think I am a great saint, But I think God has been pleased to bestow such favors upon me as will benefit myself and others."

But when it came to discussing her manuscript she said to Pauline, "Mother, you must not discuss the manuscript with anyone until it has been published—with our Mother's [Marie de Gonzague's] consent. If you do act otherwise, the devil will employ more than one snare to prevent and injure the work of God—a work that is very important."

When her sister Celine sat reading her a conference on

eternal beatitude, suddenly Therese interrupted her—"It is not that which attracts me. It is love! To love and be loved, and to return to earth to make Love to be loved!"

It was on July 17 that she said, "I feel that my mission is about to begin; my mission of making souls love the good God as I love Him, to teach my little way to souls. If my desires receive fulfilment I shall spend my heaven on earth even until the end of time.

"Yes, I will spend my heaven doing good upon earth. That is not impossible, since from the midst of the beatific vision itself the angels watch over us. No, I shall not be able to take any rest until the end of the world, as long as there are souls to be saved."

"It is the way of spiritual childhood," she said in response to a question about her "little way." "It is the path of total abandonment and confidence. I would show them the little method I have found so perfectly successful and tell them there is but one thing to do on earth; to cast before Jesus the flowers of little sacrifices. That is what I have done and that is why I shall be so well received.

"God would not have given me the desire to do good upon earth after my death if He did not will to realize it; He would rather have given me the desire to rest in Him."

Her favorite picture of Jesus Christ was the Holy Face, the imprint made upon Veronica's veil which has often been represented.

"My devotion to the Holy Face, or rather *all my spirituality,* has been based on these words of Isaias: 'There is no beauty in him, nor comeliness; and we have seen him, and there was no sightliness in him. Despised and the most abject of men, a man of sorrows, and acquainted with infirmity; and his look was, as it were, hidden and despised, whereupon we esteemed him not.' I too desire to be without glory or beauty, to tread the winepress alone, unknown to any creature."

It was not ecstasies or visions that Therese was talking about when she spoke of dying of love. "All such fancies cannot help me; I can nourish myself only on the truth. That is the reason I have never wanted to have any visions. On earth we can never behold heaven and the angels as they really are. I much prefer to wait for that until after my death."

There has been so much discussion of the diminutive "little" which Therese used constantly that it is good to remember her words of explanation on August 6. "To be little . . . is . . . not to attribute to ourselves the virtues we practice, nor to believe ourselves capable of practicing virtue at all. It is rather to recognize the fact that God puts treasures of virtue into the hands of his little children to make use of them in time of need, but they remain always treasures of the good God. Finally, to be little means that we must never be discouraged over our faults, for children often fall but they are too small to harm themselves very much."

The total unimportance of anything in this world except God's love for us—this was the burden of her teaching. And how little He is loved in return! "How little is the good God loved upon earth, even by those who are consecrated to Him! . . . No, God is not much loved! . . ."

(If those periods mean the leaving out of other thoughts on this subject, we wish they had been left in.)

When her sisters took down her words, made note of what she said, it irked her because she could not make them understand that she herself did nothing, that it was Jesus who was patient *in her,* who endured in her from moment to moment.

Toward the end of the month of August other complications set in. "All the better, to have much to suffer on every side, and to have a variety of maladies at the same time. It is like being on a journey during which we valiantly put up with all sorts of inconveniences, knowing well it will soon be over, and that once the end is attained, we will rejoice all the more. Oh Mother, what would become of me if God did not give me His strength. My hands alone are free. One would never believe it possible to suffer like this. No, it must be experienced to be understood."

When she asked for prayers to help her in her agony and

the sisters started to kneel, she told them, no, not on their knees but sitting beside her. She was hard only on herself.

Even when she was in an agony, she thought of her brothers in need. She offered her pain for a seminarian who was struggling against his vocation. Again she offered her interior trial "for a relative by marriage who has not the Faith," for a priest who had fallen away from his high calling.

Once when they were giving her news of great happenings in the world, the reception of the Czar of Russia in Paris, she said, "I am not dazzled by all that. Speak to me of God, of the examples of the saints, and of all that is the truth.

"For the rest, brethren, whatsoever things are true, whatsoever modest, whatsoever just, whatsoever holy, whatsoever lovely, whatsoever of good fame, if there be any virtue, if any praise of discipline: think on these things."

When they talked to her of Heaven she said, "If you only knew how calm the thought of going to heaven so soon leaves me. It is true I am very happy, but I cannot say I experience living joy and transports of delight, no. I tell you again, I do not prefer one thing more than another. That which God loves best and chooses for me, that is the thing which pleases me most."

She thought she had no fear of death and said so, on September 5, and said that it was with joy that she would leave the world. But by September 11 she confessed to having experienced this fear. "But I have no fear of that which comes after death and I do not regret leaving this life. Oh no, I only pondered within myself with a sort of apprehension, what is this mysterious separation of the soul from the body. It is the first time I experienced anything like that, but straightway I abandoned myself to the good God."

Whenever those around her lamented at seeing her suffer, she told them to remember that around the sick one should always be cheerful. "We must not lament as those who have no hope."

When they asked her if she had any intuition about her death: "Ah, Mother, about intuitions. If you only knew in what poverty I find myself. I know no more than you know . . . I divine nothing except what I see and hear. But my soul, notwithstanding the darkness, enjoys a most astonishing peace."

Over and over again she tried to emphasize the fact that in the spiritual life, it is not a matter of feeling, seeing, speaking, tasting. She was "only too conscious how impossible it is for human speech to put into words what the heart itself can scarcely realize. No words of earth can communicate the secrets of heaven." "After writing page after page, I should still feel I had not yet begun . . . The palette of the Divine painter will alone be able, when the night of this life has passed, to supply me with the colors needed to portray the wonders my soul descries." How to describe the things of the spirit with the tongue of flesh?

On one of the last days of her life, when she was suffering so extremely, she cried out, "Oh, what does it matter to write eloquently about suffering. Nothing. Nothing. One must have experienced actual suffering to know the value of such utterances."

Afraid, later, that she had scandalized her sister with her bitterness, she looked at Pauline "in an altogether singular manner, and pronounced these words: 'I know well now that all I have said and written is entirely true . . . It is true that I have desired to suffer much for God, and it is true that I desire it still.' "

For the next two days she could scarcely breathe, and there was a painful rattling in her throat. "How ought I to set about dying," she cried out. "I shall never know how to die."

"Is it today that I will die?" she asked the Mother Prioress and both the doctor and Mother Prioress thought that they could assure her that it would be that day. But the long day dragged through and the evening came and the work of prayer went on in the monastery until ten as usual. That night Sister Marie and Sister Genevieve (Celine) stayed with her and the next long day came, finding her utterly exhausted.

"It is all pure agony, without any admixture of consolation," she said.

All day she lay in torment and yet toward afternoon she was suddenly able to sit up in bed. "See," she said, "perhaps there are months more ahead. I do not believe it is death, but months more of suffering. And tomorrow it will be worse." But it was not a cry of despair. "Well, so much the better."

In the afternoon she begged Mother Prioress to help her to prepare for death. "Prepare me to die well." And later, "All that I have written about my desire for suffering, oh yes, it is quite true!"

"I do not repent of having delivered myself up to Love."

She had offered herself a victim of Love rather than of Justice, offering herself on behalf of all those who rejected Christ's love. "All my smallest desires have been realized . . . Then the greatest of all, *to die of love,* must also be realized."

On September 30, for two hours, from five o'clock until seven o'clock, with many of the sisters of the community gathered around her praying, she went through a terrible death agony. "Her features were contracted, her hands purple, her feet were icy cold and she trembled in every limb. The death sweat stood out in great drops on her forehead and coursed down her face. The ever increasing oppression made her utter feeble involuntary cries in her efforts to breathe." This is Pauline's description of the terrible ordeal. The sisters were used to long hours on their knees but thinking there would be hours yet to await the death of the young nun, the Prioress dismissed the community to go about their duties.

"Oh mother, is it not yet the agony, am I not going to die?" Therese is said to have cried out. It might be some hours yet, Mother Marie de Gonzague, who had sat by many a death bed in her community, assured her.

"Ah well! So be it! So be it! Oh, I do not wish to suffer less. Oh I love Him. My God, I love You."

These were her last words. The sisters were summoned quickly back into the infirmary to kneel about the bedside and to witness the last moments of this girl who wished to die of love. According to her sister Pauline, her face at that moment suddenly lost all look of suffering and there was a sudden blooming, a sudden joy transforming her.

"Her gaze remaining fixed on high, irradiated, and expressed such happiness as surpassed all her desires. She made certain movements with her head as though at intervals she was being divinely wounded by the shafts of love. Immediately after that ecstasy, which lasted for the space of a Credo, she closed her eyes and breathed her last sigh.

"That was at about twenty minutes past seven o'clock. Our holy little sister preserved in death an ineffable smile and was of a ravishing beauty."

When her sisters prepared her for burial they remarked to the infirmarian "how very young Therese appeared, so that we should not have thought her more than a girl twelve or thirteen years of age. . . ."

"I should like to mention here two other circumstances that marked the evening of September 30," Sister Pauline whose notes these are, concluded. "During the long agony of St. Therese of the Child Jesus, a multitude of little birds took their station on a tree beside the wide open window of the Infirmary, where they continued to sing with all their might until her death. Never before had there been such a concert in the garden. I was rather depressed by the contrast between so much suffering within and the joyous notes without . . . And although September 30, 1897, had been a dark and rainy day, nevertheless, towards seven o'clock in the evening, the clouds all dispersed with surpassing rapidity and soon the stars were shining in a bright, clear sky."

XVIII

The Shower of Roses

How are saints canonized by the Church? In a sense, when we are in a state of grace, when there is no mortal sin on our souls, we are all saints. St. Paul in his Epistles used to address his followers as "saints," or as "called to be saints." The Mormons called themselves a Church of Latter Day Saints. "This is the will of God, your sanctification," St. Paul wrote.

A holy and practical monsignor in Paris said once that two things were necessary to make a saint, money and miracles, and St. Therese sent both. If she wished her *way* to be known, if she wished her message to be heard, it was her responsibility to provide both. So shortly after her death the rain of roses began: cures of cancer, tuberculosis, nephritis, and all manner of painful and mortal diseases. Nuns in need of money to pay off the mortgages on their schools, hospitals and orphanages found it appearing, sometimes in the form of gifts, sometimes carefully placed in a desk drawer. When Therese healed a little Irish child, she appeared to her as a little child in her First Communion frock, and shook hands with her as she left, and the radiant little patient who had been unconscious and at the brink of death, sat up and told her mother to bring her her clothes, and food because she was starving. Soldiers saw Therese on the battlefield; she walked in Paris; she appeared to the sick. "After my death I will let fall a shower of roses," she had said, and sometimes

172

the roses appeared literally, and sometimes just the fragrance of them.

Her little book, *The Story of a Soul,* appeared first in French in 1898, a year after her death, and then it was translated by a Polish teacher, living in Prague, into English, and from then on new translations were always appearing. Cardinal Dougherty of Philadelphia said that he came across translations into Japanese, into Chinese, into the languages of the Filipinos. Wherever he traveled, there was the story of this modern saint, who willed to be as obscure as "a little grain of sand" during her short life, but willed equally vigorously to be known when she died. Her mission was then to begin, she said, and she would not rest until the end of the world.

Therese Martin died on September 30, 1897. Only seventeen years later, when those who had been born in the same year with her were just forty-one years of age, the fame of her sanctity had so spread among the people that her cause was introduced at Rome, on June 9, 1914. She was beatified on April 29, 1923, and canonized on May 17, 1925, an unusually rapid process for the Church in modern times.

So many books have been written about St. Therese, books of all kinds, too, so why, I ask myself again, have I written one more? There are popular lives, lives written for children, travelogue lives following her footsteps, lives for the extrovert, the introvert, the contemplative, the activist, the scholar and the theologian.

Yet it was the "worker," the common man, who first spread her fame by word of mouth. It was the masses who first proclaimed her a saint. It was the "people."

When we think of the masses, we think of waves of the sea, of forests, of fields of wheat, all moved by the spirit which blows where it listeth. When we think of the people we think of the child at school, the housewife at her dishpan, the mother working, the mother sick, the man traveling, the migrant worker, the craftsman, the factory worker, the soldier, the rich, the bourgeois, the poor in tenements, the destitute man in the street. To a great extent she has made her appeal to all of these.

What was there about her to make such an appeal? Perhaps because she was so much like the rest of us in her ordinariness. In her lifetime there are no miracles recounted, she was just good, good as the bread which the Normans bake in huge loaves, and which makes up a large part of their diet. Good as the pale cider which takes the place of the wine of the rest of France, since Normandy is an apple country. "Small beer," one might say. She compares to the great saints, as cider compares with wine, others might complain. But it is the world itself which has canonized her, it is the common people who have taken her to their hearts. And now the theologians are writing endlessly to explain how big she was, and not little, how mature and strong she was, not childlike and dependent. They are tired of hearing people couple her name with that of Teresa of Avila whom they call the "Great Teresa" as distinguished from the "Little Therese."

What did she do? She practiced the presence of God and she did all things—all the little things that make up our daily life and contact with others—for His honor and glory. She did not need much time to expound what she herself called "her little way," which she said was for all. She wrote her story, and God did the rest. God and the people. God chose for the people to clamor for her canonization.

What stands out in her life? Her holiness of course, and the holiness of her entire family. That is not an ordinary thing in this day of post-war materialism, delinquency and all those other words which indicate how dissatisfied the world of the West is with its economy of abundance while the world of the East sits like Lazarus at the gate of Dives.

With governments becoming stronger and more centralized, the common man feels his ineffectiveness. When the whole world seems given over to preparedness for war and the show of force, the message of Therese is quite a different one.

She speaks to our condition. Is the atom a small thing?

And yet what havoc it has wrought. Is her little way a small contribution to the life of the spirit? It has all the power of the spirit of Christianity behind it. It is an explosive force that can transform our lives and the life of the world, once put into effect. In the homily he gave after the Gospel at the Mass of her canonization, Pope Pius XI said: "If the way of spiritual childhood became general, who does not see how easily would be realized the reformation of human society. . . ."

The seeds of this teaching are being spread, being broadcast, to be watered by our blood perhaps, but with a promise of a harvest. God will give the increase. At a time when there are such grave fears because of the radioactive particles that are sprinkled over the world by the hydrogen bomb tests, and the question is asked, what effect they are going to have on the physical life of the universe, one can state that this saint, of this day, is releasing a force, a spiritual force, upon the world to counteract that fear and that disaster. We know that one impulse of grace is of infinitely more power than a cobalt bomb. Therese has said, "All is grace."

She declared, "I will spend my heaven doing good upon earth." "I will raise up a mighty host of little saints." "My mission is to make God loved, to make Love loved."

And one can only remember the story of Abraham and how he asked, "Wilt thou destroy the just with the wicked? If there be fifty just men in the city, shall they perish withal? And wilt thou not spare that place for the sake of the fifty just, if they be therein? Far be it from thee to do this thing, and to slay the just with the wicked, and for the just to be in like case as the wicked. This is not beseeming thee: Thou, who judgest all the earth, wilt not make this judgment."

The mystery of suffering has a different aspect under the New Covenant, since Christ died on the Cross and took on Himself men's sins. Now St. Paul teaches that we can fill up the sufferings of Christ, that we must share in the sufferings of the world to lessen them, to show our love for our brothers. But God does not change, so we can trust with Abraham that for even ten just men, He will not destroy the city. We can look with faith and hope to that *mighty army of little ones* that St. Therese has promised us and which is present now among us.

At the time the Basilica in Lisieux was blessed, Pope Pius XII, then Cardinal Pacelli, said:

> The dazzling genius of Augustine, the luminous wisdom of Thomas Aquinas, have shed forth upon souls the rays of an imperishable splendor; through them, Christ and His doctrine have become better known. The divine poem lived out by Francis of Assisi has given to the world an imitation, as yet unequaled, of the life of God made man. Through him legions of men and women have learned to love God more perfectly. But a little Carmelite who had hardly reached adult age has conquered in less than half a century innumerable hosts of disciples. Doctors of the law have become children at her school; the Supreme Shepherd has exalted her and prays to her with humble and assiduous supplications; and even at this moment from one end of the earth to the other, there are millions of souls whose interior life has received the beneficent influence of the little book, *The Autobiography*.

These strong words from Pope Pius XII, a man born just three years after St. Therese, give a remarkable perspective on the humble soul who, when she was a twenty-year-old nun in the Carmel at Lisieux and he was a seventeen-year-old student in Rome, wrote in a letter to her sister Celine, "Few are the souls that aspire to be lonely and unknown."